SQL
Server

If you have any questions, comments, or feedback about this book, I would love to hear from you.

Please feel free to reach out to me via email:

Email: ec.books.contact@gmail.com

Table of Contents

Info

The code in this guide was tested on SQL Server 2022.

There may be certain syntax, code constructs, or concepts that are not explained in some topics, but they will be discussed later to avoid confusing the reader.

This book is written in a minimalistic style and follows a logical flow of topics, allowing you to write programs quickly without unnecessary delays.

SQL Server Introduction

SQL, or Structured Query Language, is a domain-specific language used for managing and manipulating relational databases. It provides a standardized way to interact with databases, enabling users to perform various operations such as querying data, updating records, inserting new data, and deleting information. SQL is a fundamental tool for anyone working with databases, and it is supported by most relational database management systems (RDBMS), including MySQL, PostgreSQL, SQLite, Oracle, and more.

SQL Server is a relational database management system (RDBMS) developed by Microsoft. It is a solution that is widely used for storing, managing, and retrieving data.

A relational database is a type of database that stores and organizes data in tables with rows and columns.

Transact-SQL (T-SQL) is Microsoft's extension of SQL (Structured Query Language) used with Microsoft SQL Server and Azure SQL Database. T-SQL includes additional features and capabilities beyond the standard SQL, making it a powerful language for managing and querying relational databases.

Why use SQL?

Storing data in a SQL database offers several advantages that make it a preferred choice for many applications.

Here are some reasons why storing data in a SQL database is beneficial:

Data Integrity: SQL databases enforce data integrity through constraints (such as primary keys, foreign keys, and unique constraints), ensuring that the data is accurate, consistent, and follows predefined rules.

Scalability: SQL databases can handle large amounts of data and scale horizontally (across multiple servers) or vertically (on a single server). This scalability is important for applications that need to grow and handle increasing amounts of data.

Data Security: SQL databases offer robust security features, including authentication, authorization, and encryption. Access to data can be restricted at various levels, ensuring that only authorized users have the appropriate permissions.

Indexing and Performance: SQL databases support indexing, which can significantly improve query performance by allowing the database engine to locate and retrieve data more efficiently.

Backup and Recovery: SQL databases provide tools and mechanisms for regular data backups and recovery, ensuring that data can be restored in case of accidental deletion, hardware failures, or other issues.

Concurrency Control: SQL databases implement mechanisms for managing concurrent access to the database, ensuring that multiple users can interact with the data simultaneously without compromising its integrity.

Development Environment

To develop with, you'll need a code development environment.

1. SQL Server

   https://www.microsoft.com/en-us/sql-server/sql-server-downloads

2. SSMS (SQL Server Management Studio) - a graphical user interface (GUI) tool provided by Microsoft for managing and interacting with SQL Server databases.

   https://learn.microsoft.com/en-us/sql/ssms

3. Visual Studio - the official IDE for C# applications that work with SQL Server

   https://visualstudio.microsoft.com/downloads

Reserved Keywords

In SQL Server, there are reserved keywords that have specific meanings and functionalities within the SQL language. These keywords are reserved for use as identifiers, and they cannot be used as names for tables, columns, or other database objects unless enclosed in square brackets or double quotes.

It's important to be aware of these keywords to avoid conflicts when naming your database objects. If you need to use a reserved keyword as an identifier, you can enclose it in square brackets, like [SELECT] or [select]. However, it's generally a good practice to avoid using reserved keywords as identifiers to prevent confusion and improve code readability.

ADD, EXTERNAL, PROCEDURE, ALL, FETCH, PUBLIC, ALTER, FILE, RAISERROR, AND, FILLFACTOR, READ, ANY, FOR, READTEXT, AS, FOREIGN, RECONFIGURE, ASC, FREETEXT, REFERENCES, AUTHORIZATION, FREETEXTTABLE, REPLICATION, BACKUP, FROM, RESTORE, BEGIN, FULL, RESTRICT, BETWEEN, FUNCTION, RETURN, BREAK, GOTO, REVERT, BROWSE, GRANT, REVOKE, BULK, GROUP, RIGHT, BY, HAVING, ROLLBACK, CASCADE, HOLDLOCK, ROWCOUNT, CASE, IDENTITY, ROWGUIDCOL, CHECK, IDENTITY_INSERT, RULE, CHECKPOINT, IDENTITYCOL, SAVE, CLOSE, IF, SCHEMA, CLUSTERED, IN, SECURITYAUDIT, COALESCE, INDEX, SELECT, COLLATE, INNER, SEMANTICKEYPHRASETABLE, COLUMN, INSERT, SEMANTICSIMILARITYDETAILSTABLE, COMMIT, INTERSECT, SEMANTICSIMILARITYTABLE, COMPUTE, INTO, SESSION_USER, CONSTRAINT, IS, SET, CONTAINS, JOIN, SETUSER, CONTAINSTABLE, KEY, SHUTDOWN, CONTINUE, KILL, SOME, CONVERT, LEFT, STATISTICS, CREATE, LIKE, SYSTEM_USER, CROSS, LINENO, TABLE, CURRENT, LOAD, TABLESAMPLE, CURRENT_DATE, MERGE, TEXTSIZE, CURRENT_TIME, NATIONAL, THEN, CURRENT_TIMESTAMP, NOCHECK, TO, CURRENT_USER, NONCLUSTERED, TOP, CURSOR, NOT, TRAN, DATABASE, NULL, TRANSACTION, DBCC, NULLIF, TRIGGER, DEALLOCATE, OF, TRUNCATE, DECLARE, OFF, TRY_CONVERT, DEFAULT, OFFSETS, TSEQUAL, DELETE, ON, UNION, DENY, OPEN, UNIQUE, DESC, OPENDATASOURCE, UNPIVOT, DISK, OPENQUERY, UPDATE, DISTINCT, OPENROWSET, UPDATETEXT, DISTRIBUTED, OPENXML, USE, DOUBLE, OPTION, USER, DROP, OR, VALUES, DUMP, ORDER, VARYING, ELSE, OUTER, VIEW, END, OVER, WAITFOR, ERRLVL, PERCENT, WHEN, ESCAPE, PIVOT, WHERE, EXCEPT, PLAN, WHILE, EXEC, PRECISION, WITH, EXECUTE, PRIMARY, WITHIN, EXISTS, PRINT,

WRITETEXT, EXIT, PROC, ABSOLUTE, OVERLAPS, ACTION, PAD, ADA, PARTIAL, PASCAL, EXTRACT, POSITION, ALLOCATE, FALSE, PREPARE, FIRST, PRESERVE, FLOAT, ARE, PRIOR, PRIVILEGES, FORTRAN, ASSERTION, FOUND, AT, REAL, AVG, GET, GLOBAL, RELATIVE, GO, BIT, BIT_LENGTH, BOTH, ROWS, HOUR, CASCADED, SCROLL, IMMEDIATE, SECOND, CAST, SECTION, CATALOG, INCLUDE, CHAR, SESSION, CHAR_LENGTH, INDICATOR, CHARACTER, INITIALLY, CHARACTER_LENGTH, SIZE, INPUT, SMALLINT, INSENSITIVE, SPACE, INT, SQL, COLLATION, INTEGER, SQLCA, SQLCODE, INTERVAL, SQLERROR, CONNECT, SQLSTATE, CONNECTION, SQLWARNING, ISOLATION, SUBSTRING, CONSTRAINTS, SUM, LANGUAGE, CORRESPONDING, LAST, TEMPORARY, COUNT, LEADING, TIME, LEVEL, TIMESTAMP, TIMEZONE_HOUR, LOCAL, TIMEZONE_MINUTE, LOWER, MATCH, TRAILING, MAX, MIN, TRANSLATE, DATE, MINUTE, TRANSLATION, DAY, MODULE, TRIM, MONTH, TRUE, DEC, NAMES, DECIMAL, NATURAL, UNKNOWN, NCHAR, DEFERRABLE, NEXT, UPPER, DEFERRED, NO, USAGE, NONE, USING, DESCRIBE, VALUE, DESCRIPTOR, DIAGNOSTICS, NUMERIC, VARCHAR, DISCONNECT, OCTET_LENGTH, DOMAIN, ONLY, WHENEVER, WORK, END-EXEC, WRITE, YEAR, OUTPUT, ZONE, EXCEPTION, HOST, RELEASE, ADMIN, IGNORE, RESULT, AFTER, RETURNS, AGGREGATE, ROLE, ALIAS, INITIALIZE, ROLLUP, ROUTINE, INOUT, ROW, ARRAY, ASENSITIVE, SAVEPOINT, ASYMMETRIC, INTERSECTION, SCOPE, SEARCH, ATOMIC, BEFORE, ITERATE, BINARY, SENSITIVE, LARGE, SEQUENCE, BLOB, BOOLEAN, LATERAL, SETS, SIMILAR, BREADTH, LESS, CALL, CALLED, LIKE_REGEX, CARDINALITY, LIMIT, SPECIFIC, LN, SPECIFICTYPE, LOCALTIME, SQLEXCEPTION, LOCALTIMESTAMP, LOCATOR, CLASS, MAP, START, CLOB, STATE, MEMBER, STATEMENT, COLLECT, METHOD, STATIC, COMPLETION, STDDEV_POP, CONDITION, MOD, STDDEV_SAMP, MODIFIES, STRUCTURE, MODIFY, SUBMULTISET, SUBSTRING_REGEX, CONSTRUCTOR, SYMMETRIC, CORR, MULTISET, SYSTEM, COVAR_POP, TERMINATE, COVAR_SAMP, THAN, CUBE, NCLOB, CUME_DIST, NEW, CURRENT_CATALOG, CURRENT_DEFAULT_TRANSFORM_GROUP, CURRENT_PATH, CURRENT_ROLE, NORMALIZE, TRANSLATE_REGEX, CURRENT_SCHEMA, CURRENT_TRANSFORM_GROUP_FOR_TYPE, OBJECT, TREAT, CYCLE, OCCURRENCES_REGEX, DATA, OLD, UESCAPE, UNDER, OPERATION, ORDINALITY, UNNEST, OUT, OVERLAY, DEPTH, VAR_POP, DEREF, PARAMETER, VAR_SAMP, PARAMETERS, VARIABLE, DESTROY, PARTITION, DESTRUCTOR, PATH, WIDTH_BUCKET, DETERMINISTIC, POSTFIX, WITHOUT, DICTIONARY, PREFIX, WINDOW, PREORDER, PERCENT_RANK, DYNAMIC,

PERCENTILE_CONT, XMLAGG, EACH, PERCENTILE_DISC,
XMLATTRIBUTES, ELEMENT, POSITION_REGEX, XMLBINARY, XMLCAST,
EQUALS, XMLCOMMENT, EVERY, XMLCONCAT, RANGE,
XMLDOCUMENT, READS, XMLELEMENT, FILTER, XMLEXISTS,
RECURSIVE, XMLFOREST, REF, XMLITERATE, REFERENCING,
XMLNAMESPACES, FREE, REGR_AVGX, XMLPARSE, FULLTEXTTABLE,
REGR_AVGY, XMLPI, FUSION, REGR_COUNT, XMLQUERY, GENERAL,
REGR_INTERCEPT, XMLSERIALIZE, REGR_R2, XMLTABLE,
REGR_SLOPE, XMLTEXT, REGR_SXX, XMLVALIDATE, GROUPING,
REGR_SXY, HOLD, REGR_SYY

Case Sensitivity

In SQL Server, the case sensitivity of identifiers (such as table names, column names, and variable names) and string comparison is determined by the collation settings.

Case Sensitivity in Commands

The case sensitivity of SQL commands, such as SELECT and select, is generally not significant in SQL Server. SQL Server is not case-sensitive for keywords, which means that you can write SQL commands using uppercase, lowercase, or a mix of both, and they will be interpreted the same way.

Case Sensitivity in Identifiers

Server-Level Collation:

When you install SQL Server, you choose a default collation for the entire server. This server-level collation setting can be case-sensitive or case-insensitive.

If the server collation is case-sensitive, identifiers are treated as case-sensitive.

If the server collation is case-insensitive, identifiers are treated as case-insensitive.

Database-Level Collation:

Each database within a SQL Server instance can have its own collation setting, which can override the server-level collation.

If the database collation is case-sensitive, identifiers within that database are treated as case-sensitive.

If the database collation is case-insensitive, identifiers within that database are treated as case-insensitive.

Create Database

Install SQL Server and SSMS.

Open SSMS and connect to your local database:

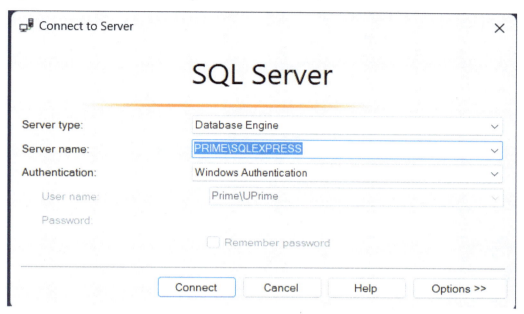

Create new database:

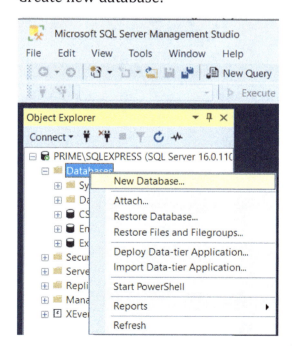

Pick database name and press ok:

Right-click on the newly created database and select "New Query".

You use this window to create, modify, and execute SQL queries.

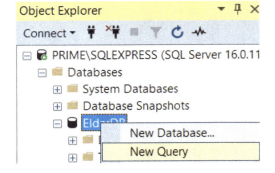

Data types

SQL Server supports a variety of data types to store different types of data. Data types are used to define the type of data that can be stored in a column in a table or in a parameter of a stored procedure or function.

When you declare a variable, you typically use the DECLARE statement followed by the variable name, its data type, and any initial value. The @ symbol is used to denote variables. They are prefixed with @ to distinguish them from column names, table names, or other identifiers.

```
DECLARE @myVar INT;
```

In this example, @myVar is a variable of type INT, which can store integer values.

Exact numerics

TINYINT/INT/SMALLINT/BIGINT

Numeric data types are used to store numeric values with different levels of precision and scale.

Data type	Range	Range expression	Storage
tinyint	0 to 255	2^0-1 to 2^8-1	1 Byte
int	-2,147,483,648 to 2,147,483,647	-2^31 to 2^31-1	4 Bytes
smallint	-32,768 to 32,767	-2^15 to 2^15-1	2 Bytes
bigint	-9,223,372,036,854,775,808 to 9,223,372,036,854,775,807	-2^63 to 2^63-1	8 Bytes

```
DECLARE @tinyInt TINYINT = 127
DECLARE @int INT = 2147483647
DECLARE @smallInt SMALLINT = -32768
DECLARE @bigInt BIGINT = 9223372036854775807
```

MONEY/SMALLMONEY

Data types that represent monetary or currency values. The money data type is specifically designed for handling monetary values. It provides a fixed-point data type with precision suitable for financial calculations involving currency.

Data type	Range	Storage
smallmoney	-214,748.3648 to 214,748.3647	4 bytes
money	-922,337,203,685,477.5808 to 922,337,203,685,477.5807 (-922,337,203,685,477.58 to 922,337,203,685,477.58 for Informatica. Informatica only supports two decimals, not four.)	8 bytes

```
DECLARE @money MONEY = 12345.67
DECLARE @smallMoney SMALLMONEY = 123.45
```

DECIMAL/NUMERIC

The decimal and numeric data types are functionally identical. The numeric data type is an older synonym for the decimal data type, and it is still supported in SQL Server for backward compatibility.

```
DECLARE @myDecimal1 decimal(5,2) = 12.34;
DECLARE @myDecimal2 decimal(10,5) = 123.45678;
DECLARE @myDecimal3 decimal(38,0) = 1000000000000000000;
```

Data Type	Precision	Scale	Range	Storage
decimal	Up to 38	Up to 38	±10^28 - 1	16 bytes
numeric	Up to 38	Up to 127	(User-specified)	Up to 17 bytes

The decimal[(p[,s])] and numeric[(p[,s])] data types in SQL Server represent fixed-precision and scale numbers. The p parameter specifies the precision, which is the total number of digits that can be stored in the data type. The s parameter specifies the scale, which is the number of digits to the right of the decimal point.

Precision	Storage bytes
1 - 9	5
10-19	9
20-28	13
29-38	17

The p (precision) parameter specifies the maximum total number of decimal digits that can be stored in the data type. This number includes both the left and the right sides of the decimal point. The precision must be a value from 1 through the maximum precision of 38. The default precision is 18.

The s (scale) parameter specifies the number of decimal digits that are stored to the right of the decimal point. This number is subtracted from p to determine the maximum number of digits to the left of the decimal point. scale must be a value from 0 through p, and can only be specified if precision is specified. The default scale is 0 and so 0 <= s <= p. Maximum storage sizes vary, based on the precision.

When you declare the decimal or numeric data type without explicitly specifying the precision (p) and scale (s), the default values are used. The default precision is 18, and the default scale is 0.

```
decimal = decimal(18,0)
```

BIT

The bit is an integer data type that can store only two values: 0 and 1. It is used to represent Boolean values, which are true/false values. The bit is the smallest integer data type and occupies 1 byte of storage space.

```
DECLARE @bit BIT = 1
DECLARE @bit2 BIT = 0
```

Approximate numerics

FLOAT/REAL

The float[(n)] data type in SQL Server allows you to specify the precision of a floating-point number by specifying the number of bits used to store its mantissa. The mantissa is the part of a floating-point number that represents the significant digits of the value. The precision of a floating-point number determines the number of significant digits that can be accurately represented by the number.

```
DECLARE @real REAL = 123.456
DECLARE @float FLOAT = 12345.6789
```

Data type	Range	Storage
float	- 1.79E+308 to -2.23E-308, 0 and 2.23E-308 to 1.79E+308	Depends on the value of n
real	- 3.40E + 38 to -1.18E - 38, 0 and 1.18E - 38 to 3.40E + 38	4 Bytes

n value	Precision	Storage size
1-24	7 digits	4 bytes
25-53	15 digits	8 bytes

when you use the float data type without specifying a precision (commonly denoted as float without (n)), it usually defaults to a double-precision floating-point number. A float without specifying (n) is equivalent to float(53).

```
float = float(53)
```

Approximate Numerics vs Exact Numerics

Approximate Numerics

Floating-Point Representation: Approximate numerics use a floating-point representation, which means they store values as approximations and don't always represent them with exact precision.

Limited Precision: Due to the nature of floating-point arithmetic, there can be rounding errors and loss of precision during calculations.

Use Cases: Typically used in scenarios where an exact representation is not crucial, and a wider range of values is needed. Commonly used in scientific calculations or situations where precision limitations are acceptable.

Exact Numerics

Fixed Precision and Scale: Exact numerics use fixed precision and scale. Precision specifies the total number of digits, and scale indicates the number of digits to the right of the decimal point.

No Rounding During Operations: Exact numerics do not involve rounding during storage or arithmetic operations. The results of calculations are precise and maintain the specified precision and scale.

Use Cases: Suitable for scenarios where precision is critical, such as in financial applications, where rounding errors could lead to significant discrepancies.

In this example, @approximateValue is an approximate numeric, and @exactValue is an exact numeric. The result stored in @exactValue will be precise according to the specified precision and scale, while @approximateValue may store an approximate result due to the nature of floating-point representation.

```
-- Approximate Numeric
DECLARE @approximateValue FLOAT = 123.456789 / 3.0
-- The result may be a rounded approximation

-- Exact Numeric
DECLARE @exactValue DECIMAL(10, 2) = 123.456789 / 3.0
-- The result is precise with fixed precision and scale
```

Character strings

Character strings are used to store character string data.

Strings in SQL are typically denoted by single quotes 'MyString'.

CHAR/VARCHAR

CHAR and VARCHAR are both used to store character string data, but there are some key differences between them.

char(n) - fixed-length data type.

varchar (n | max) - variable-length data type.

n - defines the string size in bytes and must be a value from 1 - 8,000.

max - defines a column constraint size up to a maximum storage of 2^31-1 bytes (2 GB).

```
DECLARE @myChar CHAR(10) = 'abc'
DECLARE @myVarchar VARCHAR(50) = 'abc'
DECLARE @myVarcharMax VARCHAR(MAX) = 'abc'
```

If you omit the precision for both the CHAR and VARCHAR variables, the length of the variables will be 1.

```
DECLARE @myChar CHAR = 'abc';
SELECT @myChar --Output: a
```

In this case, the precision will be a

Fixed vs Variable Length

CHAR: It is a fixed-length data type. When you define a column as CHAR(10), for example, it will always reserve space for 10 characters, regardless of the actual length of the data stored in the column. If you store a string "hello" in a CHAR(10) column, it will be stored as "hello " (padded with spaces to fill the remaining characters).

VARCHAR: It is a variable-length data type. It only stores the actual characters entered, without padding. If you store the same "hello" string in a VARCHAR(10) column, it will be stored as "hello".

Storage Space

CHAR: It tends to use more storage space because it reserves space for the maximum length of the data, even if the actual data is shorter.

VARCHAR: It is more storage-efficient since it only uses the space required for the actual data plus a small overhead (typically 2 bytes) to store the length information. The length information helps SQL Server know the size of the data when reading it. If you later assign a longer string, SQL Server allocates additional space to accommodate the new data and its length prefix.

Performance

CHAR: Retrieving data from CHAR columns might be faster in some cases, especially for fixed-length data, as the database engine can calculate offsets more easily.

VARCHAR: It might be more suitable for variable-length data and can be more storage-efficient, but there could be a slight performance overhead due to variable-length storage.

Feature	CHAR	VARCHAR
Length	Fixed	Variable
Padding	Yes	No
Storage	Maximum length	Actual length
Performance	Generally faster	Generally slower

TEXT

The TEXT data type is a deprecated data type that was used to store large amounts of non-Unicode text data. It was removed in SQL Server 2012 and replaced by the NVARCHAR(MAX) data type.

The TEXT is invalid for local variables. Use it only as a column in a table.

Unicode character strings

Unicode character strings are sequences of characters encoded using the Unicode standard. Unicode is a character encoding standard that aims to represent every character from every writing system in the world. It provides a unique numeric code point for each character, ensuring a standardized representation across different platforms and languages.

In the context of programming and databases, when we refer to Unicode character strings, we usually mean sequences of characters encoded using Unicode encodings, such as UTF-8, UTF-16, or UTF-32. These encodings define how characters are represented in memory or in storage.

UTF-8 (8-bit Unicode Transformation Format): Uses variable-length encoding, with each character represented by one to four bytes.

UTF-16 (16-bit Unicode Transformation Format): Uses variable-length encoding, with each character represented by one or two 16-bit code units.

UTF-32 (32-bit Unicode Transformation Format): Uses fixed-length encoding, with each character represented by a single 32-bit code unit.

NCHAR/NVARCHAR/N

NCHAR and NVARCHAR are data types used to store Unicode character data.

nchar(n) - fixed-length data type.

nvarchar (n | max) - variable-length data type.

n - defines the string size in bytes and must be a value from 1 - 4,000.

max - defines a column constraint size up to a maximum storage of 2^31-1 bytes (2 GB).

```
DECLARE @myNChar NCHAR(10) = N'你好';
DECLARE @myNChar2 NCHAR(10) = '你好';
DECLARE @myNVarChar NVARCHAR(10) = N'你好';
DECLARE @myNVarCharMax NVARCHAR(MAX) = N'你好';
```

N'你好': This represents a Unicode string literal. The N prefix indicates that the following string is in Unicode. When you use N'你好', each character in the string is represented using two bytes.

'你好': This represents a non-Unicode string literal (regular string literal without the N prefix). In this case, each character in the string is represented using a single byte.

If you attempt to store Unicode characters directly in a CHAR variable, SQL Server will implicitly convert them to the default character set of your database, which might result in data loss or incorrect representation, especially for non-ASCII characters.

Feature	NCHAR	NVARCHAR
Length	Fixed	Variable
Maximum length	8,000 bytes	4,000 characters
Storage efficiency	Less efficient for variable-length strings	More efficient for variable-length strings

String length

Definition of n in CHAR and VARCHAR

In CHAR(n) and VARCHAR(n), the n defines the string length in bytes, not the number of characters that can be stored.

This is consistent with the definition of NCHAR(n) and NVARCHAR(n).

Misconception with Single-Byte Encoding

The misconception often arises because, in single-byte encoding, the storage size of CHAR and VARCHAR is indeed n bytes, and the number of characters is also n.

However, with multibyte encodings like UTF-8, a single character can use two or more bytes, leading to a difference in the number of characters that can be stored.

Example with Multibyte Encoding (UTF-8)

For example, in a column defined as CHAR(10), the Database Engine can store 10 characters that use single-byte encoding (Unicode range 0 to 127). However, with multibyte encoding (Unicode range 128 to 1,114,111), fewer than 10 characters may be stored in the same space.

Default Length and Collation

When n isn't specified in a data definition or variable declaration statement, the default length is 1.

If n isn't specified with the CAST and CONVERT functions, the default length is 30.

Objects using CHAR or VARCHAR are assigned the default collation of the database unless a specific collation is assigned using the COLLATE clause. The collation controls the code page used to store the character data.

NTEXT

The NTEXT data type has been deprecated, and its use is not recommended. Microsoft recommends using the NVARCHAR (MAX) data type instead. The ntext data type was designed for storing variable-length Unicode character data of varying lengths, but it has limitations and is not as flexible or efficient as the NVARCHAR(MAX) data type. The NTEXT data type is invalid for local variables. Use it only as a column in a table.

Binary strings

Binary strings are sequences of binary data, which can include anything from raw binary files (like images or executables).

BINARY/VARBINARY

BINARY and VARBINARY data types are used to store binary data.

binary(n) - fixed-length data type.

varbinary(n | max) - variable-length data type.

n - defines the string size in bytes and must be a value from 1 - 8,000.

max - defines a column constraint size up to a maximum storage of 2^31-1 bytes (2 GB).

```
DECLARE @myBinary BINARY(5) = 0x0102030405;
DECLARE @myVarbinary VARBINARY(10) = 0x0102030405;
DECLARE @myVarbinaryMax VARBINARY(MAX) = 0x0102030405;
```

The **0x** prefix is used to denote a hexadecimal literal.

IMAGE

The IMAGE data is a deprecated data type that was used to store variable-length binary data up to 2^31-1 bytes (2 GB). The image data type is invalid for local variables. Use it only as a column in a table.

Date and time

DATE

The DATE data type is used to store. The format for the DATE data type is 'YYYY-MM-DD'.

```
DECLARE @myDate DATE = '2023-01-15';
```

Default value: 1900-01-01

Range: 0001-01-01 through 9999-12-31

Character length: 10

Storage size: 8 bytes

TIME

The TIME data type is used to store time values. It represents a time of day in hours, minutes, seconds, and fractions of a second. The format for the TIME data type is 'HH:mm:ss.sss', where HH represents hours in 24-hour format, mm represents minutes, ss represents seconds, and sss represents fractions of a second.

```
DECLARE @myTime TIME = '15:30:15.5000000';
```

Default value: 00:00:00

Range: 00:00:00.0000000 through 23:59:59.9999999

Character length: 8 (HH:mm:ss) to 16 (HH:mm:ss.nnnnnnn)

Storage size: 5 bytes

DATETIME

The DATETIME data type is used to store both date and time values. It includes information about the year, month, day, hours, minutes, seconds, and fractions of a second. The format for the DATETIME data type is 'YYYY-MM-DD HH:mm:ss.sss', where:

```
DECLARE @myDateTime DATETIME = '2023-11-18 15:30:45.123';
```

Default value: 1900-01-01 00:00:00

Date range: 1753-01-01 through 9999-12-31

Time range: 00:00:00 through 23:59:59.997

Character length: 19 - 23

Storage size: 8 bytes

Accuracy: Rounded to increments of .000, .003, or .007 seconds

DATETIME2

The DATETIME2 data type is an extension of the DATETIME data type. Its goal is to provide a higher level of precision and a broader range for date and time values. The DATETIME2 data type includes fractional seconds with higher precision than the DATETIME data type. The format for the DATETIME2 data type is 'YYYY-MM-DD HH:mm:ss.sssssssss'

```
DECLARE @myDateTime2 DATETIME2 = '2023-11-18 15:30:45.1234567';
```

Default value: 1900-01-01 00:00:00

Date range: 0001-01-01 through 9999-12-31

Time range: 00:00:00 through 23:59:59.9999999

Character length: 19 (YYYY-MM-DD HH:mm:ss) to 27 (YYYY-MM-DD HH:mm:ss.0000000)

Storage size: 6 bytes for precision less than 3, 7 bytes for precision 3 or 4,

All other precision 8 bytes

Accuracy: 100 nanoseconds

SMALLDATETIME

The SMALLDATETIME data type is similar to the DATETIME data type but with a reduced range and precision. It's designed to store date and time values with less precision than DATETIME, which can be useful in scenarios where the specific time precision is not critical. The format for the SMALLDATETIME data type is 'YYYY-MM-DD HH:mm'.

```
DECLARE @mySmallDateTime SMALLDATETIME = '2023-11-18 15:30';
```

Default value: 1900-01-01 00:00:00

Date range: 1900-01-01 through 2079-06-06

Time range: 00:00:00 through 23:59:59

Character length: 19

Storage size: 4 bytes

Accuracy: 1 minute

DATETIMEOFFSET

The DATETIMEOFFSET data type is used to store date and time values along with time zone information. It includes information about the year, month, day, hours, minutes, seconds, fractions of a second, and the time zone offset from UTC (Coordinated Universal Time). The format for the DATETIMEOFFSET data type is 'YYYY-MM-DD HH:mm:ss.sssssssss ±hh:mm'

```
DECLARE @myDateTimeOffset DATETIMEOFFSET =
'2023-11-18 15:30:45.1234567 +03:00';
```

Default value: 1900-01-01 00:00:00 00:00

Date range: 0001-01-01 through 9999-12-31

Time range: 00:00:00 through 23:59:59.9999999

Time zone offset range: -14:00 through +14:00

Character length: 26 (YYYY-MM-DD hh:mm:ss {+|-}hh:mm) to 34 (YYYY-MM-DD hh:mm:ss.nnnnnnn {+|-}hh:mm)

Storage size: 10 bytes

Accuracy: 100 nanoseconds

UNIQUEIDENTIFIER

The UNIQUEIDENTIFIER data type is used to store a globally unique identifier (GUID). A GUID is a 128-bit integer (16 bytes) that is generated using an algorithm designed to ensure uniqueness across time and space. The format of a GUID is typically represented as a hexadecimal string in the format xxxxxxxx-xxxx-xxxx-xxxx-xxxxxxxxxxxx.

```
DECLARE @myGuid UNIQUEIDENTIFIER =
'C0C01B20-2821-4DB1-BB20-B557A961E428';
```

Comments

Adding comments to your SQL code is a good practice for enhancing code readability and providing context. Comments can be added using -- for single-line comments or /* */ for multi-line comments.

Single-line

Single-line comments start with -- and are used to explain individual lines or provide short comments.

```
-- This is a single-line comment
```

Multi-line

Multi-line comments are enclosed between /* and */ and are suitable for longer explanations.

```
/*
   This is a multi-line comment
   It provides additional details about the purpose of the
   SQL code
*/
```

Semicolon (;)

The semicolon (;) is used as a statement terminator. While not always strictly required, using semicolons to terminate SQL statements is considered good practice, especially in complex queries or when dealing with multiple statements.

```
DECLARE @myChar CHAR = 'abc';
```

In summary, while you might get away with not using semicolons in some cases, it's a good practice to include them to ensure clarity, compatibility, and adherence to future syntax requirements.

Table

A table is a fundamental database object used to store and organize data in a structured manner. Each table consists of rows and columns, where each row represents a record, and each column represents an attribute or field. Here's a basic overview of creating and working with SQL tables.

Create table

```
CREATE TABLE Users (
    UserId INT IDENTITY(1,1),
    FirstName NVARCHAR(100) NOT NULL,
    LastName NVARCHAR(100) NOT NULL,
    RegisteredDate DATETIME NOT NULL DEFAULT GETDATE(),
);
```

This script creates the Users table. Copy the script and paste it into the Query window, and press F5 or press the button ▶ Execute

Now, verify that the table has been created.

⊞ dbo.Users

⊟ 📁 Columns

    🗒 UserId (int, not null)

    🗒 FirstName (nvarchar(100), not null)

    🗒 LastName (nvarchar(100), not null)

    🗒 RegisteredDate (datetime, not null)

Columns and Data Types

Each column in a table is defined by a name and a data type.

```
FirstName NVARCHAR(100)
```

CRUD

CRUD stands for Create, Read, Update, and Delete. It represents the four basic operations that can be performed on data in a database or any persistent storage system. These operations are fundamental to database management systems and form the basis of data manipulation.

INSERT

The INSERT statement is used to add new records (rows) to a table.

```
INSERT Users
 (FirstName
 ,LastName
 ,RegisteredDate)
VALUES
 ('Eldar'
 ,'Cohen'
 ,GETUTCDATE())
```

The GETUTCDATE() function is used to get the current UTC date and time.

Ensure that the order of the columns in the INSERT INTO statement matches the order in which they are defined in the table. For example, if the order of columns in your Users table is (FirstName, LastName, RegisteredDate), your INSERT INTO statement should reflect this order.

```
--Incorrect order
INSERT Users (LastName, FirstName, RegisteredDate)
VALUES ('Eldar', 'Cohen', GETUTCDATE());
```

In this case, you're trying to insert a string ('Eldar') into the LastName column,

and (Cohen) into the FirstName column.

Insert Multiple records

You can also insert multiple records in a single INSERT statement.

```
INSERT Users
(FirstName,LastName,RegisteredDate)
VALUES
  ('Eldar','Cohen',GETUTCDATE())
 ,('David','Cohen',GETUTCDATE())
 ,('Moses','Cohen',GETUTCDATE())
```

SELECT/FROM/Asterisk (*)

The SELECT statement is used to retrieve data from one or more tables.

FROM: Specifies the table from which to retrieve the data.

Asterisk (*) Character means selects all columns from a table.

```
SELECT *
FROM Users
```

	UserId	FirstName	LastName	RegisteredDate
1	1	Eldar	Cohen	2023-11-19 06:54:44.773
2	2	David	Cohen	2023-11-19 07:05:44.577
3	3	Moses	Cohen	2023-11-19 07:05:44.577

Select Specific Columns from a Table.

```
SELECT FirstName
    ,LastName
FROM Users
```

	FirstName	LastName
1	Eldar	Cohen
2	David	Cohen
3	Moses	Cohen

TOP

The TOP clause is used to limit the number of rows returned by a SELECT query.

```
SELECT TOP 2 *
FROM Users
```

	UserId	FirstName	LastName	RegisteredDate
1	1	Eldar	Cohen	2023-11-19 06:54:44.773
2	2	David	Cohen	2023-11-19 07:05:44.577

WHERE

The WHERE clause is used to filter the rows returned by a SELECT, UPDATE, or DELETE statement based on a specified condition. It allows you to retrieve, modify, or delete only those records that meet certain criteria.

```
SELECT *
FROM Users
WHERE UserId = 1
```

	UserId	FirstName	LastName	RegisteredDate
1	1	Eldar	Cohen	2023-11-19 06:54:44.773

Select Rows Based on Multiple Conditions:

```
SELECT *
FROM Users
WHERE FirstName = 'Eldar'
  AND RegisteredDate > '2023-01-01';
```

	UserId	FirstName	LastName	RegisteredDate
1	1	Eldar	Cohen	2023-11-19 06:54:44.773

UPDATE/SET

The UPDATE statement is used to modify existing records in a table.

the SET clause is used to specify the columns you want to update along with their new values.

Updating the FirstName and LastName columns in the Users table where the UserId is equal to 2.

```
UPDATE Users
SET FirstName = 'dan'
   ,LastName = 'israel'
WHERE UserId = 2
```

	UserId	FirstName	LastName	RegisteredDate
1	2	dan	israel	2023-11-19 07:05:44.577

Omitting the WHERE clause in an UPDATE statement can lead to unintended consequences, as it would result in updating all rows in the specified table. This is often referred to as an "unconditional update" or "update without a WHERE clause."

DELETE

The DELETE statement is used to remove rows from a table based on a specified condition.

Delete the row from the Users table where the UserId is equal to 2.

```
DELETE
FROM Users
WHERE UserId = 2
```

	UserId	FirstName	LastName	RegisteredDate
1	1	Eldar	Cohen	2023-11-19 06:54:44.773
2	3	Moses	Cohen	2023-11-19 07:05:44.577

Omitting the WHERE clause in a DELETE statement can lead to unintended consequences, as it results in deleting all rows from the specified table. This is often referred to as an "unconditional delete" or "delete without a WHERE clause."

IDENTITY

IDENTITY is a property that is commonly used with a numeric column (usually an integer) to automatically generate unique, incremental values for each new row inserted into a table.

IDENTITY (seed , increment)

seed: This is the starting value for the IDENTITY column. It is the value assigned to the first row loaded into the table. The default seed value is 1.

increment: This is the incremental value added to the identity value of the previous row loaded. The default increment value is 1.

```
UserId INT IDENTITY(1,1)
```

In this case, the UserId column will be an identity column starting at 1, incrementing by 1 for each new row.

Here's a breakdown of IDENTITY(1,1):

1: The first parameter represents the seed value, which is the starting value for the identity column. In this case, it's set to 1, meaning the first generated value will be 1.

1: The second parameter represents the increment value, which is the amount by which the identity value is increased for each new row. In this case, it's also set to 1, meaning each subsequent row will have an identity value that is one greater than the previous row.

You must specify both the seed and increment or neither. If neither is specified, the default is (1,1).

```
INSERT Users
(FirstName,LastName,RegisteredDate)
VALUES
  ('Eldar','Cohen',GETUTCDATE())
 ,('David','Cohen',GETUTCDATE())
 ,('Moses','Cohen',GETUTCDATE())

SELECT *
FROM Users
```

	UserId	FirstName	LastName	RegisteredDate
1	1	Eldar	Cohen	2023-11-19 06:54:44.773
2	2	David	Cohen	2023-11-19 07:05:44.577
3	3	Moses	Cohen	2023-11-19 07:05:44.577

UserId INT IDENTITY(325,9)

In this case, the UserId column will be an identity column starting at 325, incrementing by 9 for each new row.

```sql
INSERT Users
(FirstName,LastName,RegisteredDate)
VALUES
  ('Eldar','Cohen',GETUTCDATE())
 ,('David','Cohen',GETUTCDATE())
 ,('Moses','Cohen',GETUTCDATE())

SELECT *
FROM Users
```

	UserId	FirstName	LastName	RegisteredDate
1	325	Eldar	Cohen	2023-11-19 08:17:49.190
2	334	David	Cohen	2023-11-19 08:17:49.190
3	343	Moses	Cohen	2023-11-19 08:17:49.190

IDENTITY_INSERT

If you attempt to insert a row with an explicit value for the UserId column, SQL Server will raise an error because it is an IDENTITY column.

If you need to insert explicit values, including duplicate values, into an IDENTITY column, you can use the SET IDENTITY_INSERT statement. This allows you to temporarily override the automatic incrementing behavior of the IDENTITY column.

```
SET IDENTITY_INSERT Users ON

INSERT Users
(UserId,FirstName,LastName,RegisteredDate)
VALUES
(1,'Eldar','Cohen',GETUTCDATE())
(1,'Eldar','Cohen',GETUTCDATE())

SET IDENTITY_INSERT Users OFF
```

UserId	FirstName	LastName	RegisteredDate
1	Eldar	Cohen	2023-11-19 23:02:11.033
1	Eldar	Cohen	2023-11-19 23:02:32.663

SCOPE_IDENTITY

SCOPE_IDENTITY() Returns the last identity value generated for any table in the current session and the current scope. It is generally preferred when you want to retrieve the identity value immediately after an INSERT statement.

INSERT Users (FirstName,LastName) VALUES ('Eldar','Cohen') SELECT SCOPE_IDENTITY()		(No column name)
	1	1

INSERT Users (FirstName,LastName) VALUES ('David','Cohen') SELECT SCOPE_IDENTITY()		(No column name)
	1	2

IDENT_CURRENT

IDENT_CURRENT('Users') Returns the last identity value generated for a specific table (Users in this case) across all sessions, scopes, and even if there have been no inserts into the table since the server was restarted.

SELECT IDENT_CURRENT('Users')		(No column name)
	1	2

@@IDENTITY

@@IDENTITY Returns the last identity value generated for any table in the current session, regardless of the scope.

SELECT @@IDENTITY		(No column name)
	1	2

@@ROWCOUNT

@@ROWCOUNT is a system variable that returns the number of rows affected by the last statement that was executed as an integer (int). It is often used in statements like INSERT, UPDATE, and DELETE to determine how many rows were affected by the operation.

ROWCOUNT_BIG

ROWCOUNT_BIG is similar to the @@ROWCOUNT , but it returns a value of type bigint instead of int. This allows it to handle larger result sets or operations that affect a massive number of rows.

```
SELECT ROWCOUNT_BIG();
```

NOCOUNT

The SET NOCOUNT statement is used to control the display of the count of the number of rows affected SQL statement. When SET NOCOUNT is set to OFF, the count is displayed, and when it is set to ON, the count is not displayed.

However, your statement seems to be a bit confusing because the default behavior is to have SET NOCOUNT set to OFF. If you want to turn it off explicitly, you would use SET NOCOUNT OFF, not SET NOCOUNT off.

```
SET NOCOUNT OFF;

INSERT Users(FirstName,LastName) VALUES ('2','2')
```

```
(1 row affected)
```

```
Completion time: 2023-12-10T17:50:00.6551235+02:00
```

```
SET NOCOUNT ON;

INSERT Users(FirstName,LastName) VALUES ('3','3')
```

```
Commands completed successfully.

Completion time: 2023-12-10T17:50:22.8046991+02:00
```

Constraints

Constraints define rules or conditions that data in a table must satisfy.

Default value

You can specify default values for columns. When a new row is inserted, and no value is provided for a column with a default, the default value is used.

```
RegisteredDate DATETIME NOT NULL DEFAULT GETDATE(),
```

In this case, the RegisteredDate for the new record will be set to the current date and time due to the default constraint.

GETDATE() is a built-in function that returns the current date and time of the system.

NULL/NOT NULL

NULL and NOT NULL are used to define the nullability of a column, indicating whether a column can store NULL values or not.

NULL is a special marker used to indicate that a data value does not exist in the database. It represents the absence of a value or an undefined value. NULL is different from an empty string, zero, or any other specific value; it specifically denotes the lack of a known or meaningful value.

NULL

When a column in a database table allows NULL (is nullable), it means that this column can store NULL values, indicating that the data is optional, and a value is not required for every row.

```
FirstName NVARCHAR(100) NULL,
```

When the NULL constraint is not explicitly specified for a column, the column is considered nullable by default. This means that the column can store NULL values, indicating that the data is optional, and a value is not required for every row.

NOT NULL

```
FirstName NVARCHAR(100) NOT NULL,
```

NOT NULL is used to specify that a column must contain a value, and NULL values are not allowed. Every row in the table must have a non-NULL value for a column marked as NOT NULL.

UNIQUE

A UNIQUE constraint is used to ensure that the values in a column or a combination of columns are unique across all the rows in a table. This means that no two rows can have the same values in the specified column or columns.

```
Email VARCHAR(100) UNIQUE
```

If an attempt is made to insert or update a row with values that violate the UNIQUE constraint, the database engine will raise a constraint violation error.

A column with a UNIQUE constraint can only have a single NULL value.

A UNIQUE constraint creates a unique index on the constrained column(s), which can improve the performance of queries that involve those columns.

You can have a UNIQUE constraint on a single column or a combination of columns.

```
FirstName NVARCHAR(100) NOT NULL,
LastName NVARCHAR(100) NOT NULL,
UNIQUE (FirstName, LastName)
```

CHECK

A CHECK constraint is used to specify a condition that must be true for each row in a table. It allows you to enforce business rules or conditions on the data stored in the table. If a row violates the specified condition, the CHECK constraint prevents the data modification operation (such as an INSERT or UPDATE) from succeeding.

```
Age TINYINT CHECK (Age >= 18)
```

The Age column has a CHECK constraint, ensuring that the age is equal to or greater than 18.

Condition Format

The condition specified in a CHECK constraint can be based on a single column or a combination of columns.

Logical Expressions

You can use logical expressions, comparison operators (=, <>, <, <=, >, >=), and boolean operators (AND, OR, NOT) and (LIKE, NOT, IS) and more in the condition.

Complex Conditions

Conditions can be as simple or as complex as needed to enforce specific rules. For example, you could use a CHECK constraint to ensure that a StartDate is before an EndDate or that a Category is limited to a predefined set of values.

```
CREATE TABLE MyTable (
  StartDate DATE,
  EndDate DATE,
  Category NVARCHAR(50) CHECK (Category IN
                ('Apple', 'Orange')),
  CHECK (StartDate < EndDate)
);
```

The IN operator is used to ensure that the values inserted into the Category column are limited to a specific set of values: 'Apple', 'Orange'.

Violation Handling

If an attempt is made to insert or update a row with values that violate the CHECK constraint, the database engine will raise a constraint violation error.

Constraint Name

When you define constraints, you can provide a name for the constraint to make it more readable and meaningful. The CONSTRAINT keyword is used to assign a name to a constraint.

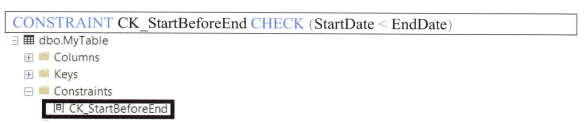

If you don't explicitly specify a name for a constraint when creating it, SQL Server will generate a system-generated name for the constraint. The generated name is typically a combination of the table name, column names, and a system-generated identifier.

Primary Key

A primary key is a unique identifier for each record in a table. It consists of one or more columns that uniquely identify a row in the table. The primary key constraint ensures that the values in the specified columns are unique and not null.

```
CREATE TABLE Users (
    UserId INT PRIMARY KEY
);
```

If you attempt to insert a record into a table with a primary key column that already exists in the table, a "Violation of PRIMARY KEY constraint" error will be raised. A primary key must be unique for each row in the table, and attempting to insert a duplicate value violates this constraint.

ORDER

When defining a primary key with ASC or DESC during table creation, it is generally used for creating a clustered index. A clustered index determines the physical order of rows on disk, impacting the storage structure.

Ascending Order (ASC): Is the default order if not specified explicitly.

Descending Order (DESC): DESC sorts the result set in descending order, meaning from the highest value to the lowest value.

```
CREATE TABLE Users (
    UserId INT
    CONSTRAINT PK_Users PRIMARY KEY(UserId DESC)
);
```

```
INSERT Users
(UserId)
VALUES
(1),(2),(3)

SELECT * FROM Users
```

	UserId
1	3
2	2
3	1

Multiple columns as primary keys

You can define a primary key constraint on multiple columns, creating a composite primary key. This means that the combination of values in these columns must be unique for each row in the table.

```sql
CREATE TABLE Users (
    FirstName NVARCHAR(50),
    LastName NVARCHAR(50),
    CONSTRAINT PK_Users PRIMARY KEY(FirstName,LastName)
);
```

FirstName and LastName columns must be unique for each row, enforcing a composite primary key.

```
⊞ dbo.Users
  ⊟ 🖿 Columns
        ⊸ FirstName (PK, nvarchar(50), not null)
        ⊸ LastName (PK, nvarchar(50), not null)
  ⊟ 🖿 Keys
        ⊸ PK_Users
```

```sql
INSERT Users
(FirstName,LastName)
VALUES
 ('Eldar','Cohen')
,('David','Cohen')

SELECT * FROM Users
```

	FirstName	LastName
1	David	Cohen
2	Eldar	Cohen

```sql
INSERT Users (FirstName,LastName) VALUES ('Eldar','Cohen')
```

This lime will raise a SQL error: Violation of PRIMARY KEY constraint 'PK_Users'. Cannot insert duplicate key in object 'dbo.Users'. The duplicate key value is (Eldar, Cohen).

Foreign Key

A foreign key is a field or a set of fields that refer to the primary key of another table. It establishes a link between two tables based on a relationship between the data in them. The table containing the foreign key is called the referencing or child table, and the table with the primary key being referred to is called the referenced or parent table.

One to many relationship

This represents a one-to-many relationship where one user can have multiple addresses.

```
CREATE TABLE Users (
    UserId BIGINT PRIMARY KEY IDENTITY(1,1),
    FirstName NVARCHAR(50),
    LastName NVARCHAR(50),
);
```

```
CREATE TABLE Addresses (
    UserId BIGINT,
    Street NVARCHAR(100),
    City NVARCHAR(100),
    Country NVARCHAR(100)

    CONSTRAINT FK_Addresses_Users FOREIGN KEY (UserId)
      REFERENCES Users(UserId)
);
```

This script creates the Addresses table with a foreign key constraint named FK_Addresses_Users, referencing the UserId column in the Users table. This establishes a relationship between the Users and Addresses tables, where the UserId in the Addresses table is a foreign key referencing the primary key in the Users table.

⊞ dbo.Addresses
□ 🗀 Columns
      ☞ UserId (FK, bigint, null)
      🗒 Street (nvarchar(100), null)
      🗒 City (nvarchar(100), null)
      🗒 Country (nvarchar(100), null)
□ 🗀 Keys
      ☞ FK_Addresses_Users

```sql
INSERT Users (FirstName,LastName)
VALUES ('Eldar','Cohen')

INSERT Addresses (UserId,Country,City)
VALUES (1,'Israel','Jerusalem'),
    (1,'Israel','Tel Aviv')

SELECT * FROM Users
SELECT * FROM Addresses
```

	UserId	FirstName	LastName
1	1	Eldar	Cohen

	UserId	Street	City	Country
1	1	NULL	Jerusalem	Israel
2	1	NULL	Tel Aviv	Israel

One to one relationship

If you want to create one-to-one relationship where one user can have only one address then use UNIQUE constraint to enforce one-to-one relationship.

```sql
CREATE TABLE Addresses (
    UserId BIGINT UNIQUE, -- one-to-one relationship
    Street NVARCHAR(100),
    City NVARCHAR(100),
    Country NVARCHAR(100)

    CONSTRAINT FK_Addresses_Users FOREIGN KEY (UserId)
     REFERENCES Users(UserId)
);
```

Delete connected row

If you want to delete a row from a table that is connected to another table through a foreign key relationship, you need to ensure that the deletion does not violate the foreign key constraint.

If you try to delete a user with UserId 1 from the Users table and there are corresponding rows in the Addresses table with UserId 1, you would get an error due to the foreign key constraint.

```
DELETE Users WHERE UserId = 1
```

The DELETE statement conflicted with the REFERENCE constraint "FK_Addresses_Users". The conflict occurred in database "EldarDB", table "dbo.Addresses", column 'UserId'

If you want to handle this situation, you need to delete addresses before deleting the user.

```
DELETE Addresses WHERE UserId = 1
DELETE Users WHERE UserId = 1
```

ON DELETE CASCADE

When you define the foreign key constraint, you can specify ON DELETE CASCADE. This means that when you delete a user from the Users table, all associated addresses in the Addresses table will be automatically deleted.

```
CONSTRAINT FK_Addresses_Users FOREIGN KEY (UserId)
  REFERENCES Users(UserId) ON DELETE CASCADE
```

ALTER

The ALTER TABLE statement is used to modify an existing table structure. This can involve changing column data types, modifying constraints, or renaming columns.

ADD

The ADD keyword is used within the context of the ALTER TABLE statement to modify the structure of an existing table by adding new elements or constraints.

Adding a New Column

```
ALTER TABLE Users
ADD Email NVARCHAR(100)
```

Adding a primary key to an existing column

```
ALTER TABLE Users
ADD PRIMARY KEY (UserId)
```

Adding a Constraint

```
ALTER TABLE Users
ADD CONSTRAINT CHK_EmailFormat CHECK (Email LIKE '%@%');
```

Adding a Default Value to an Existing Column

```
ALTER TABLE Users
ADD CONSTRAINT DF_LastName DEFAULT 'Unknown' FOR LastName;
```

The FOR keyword is used to specify the column to which the default constraint is applied.

Adding a Foreign Key

```
ALTER TABLE Addresses
ADD CONSTRAINT FK_Addresses_Users FOREIGN KEY (UserId)
 REFERENCES Users(UserId);
```

DROP

The DROP statement is used to remove database objects, such as tables, views, indexes, or constraints.

Drop a Database

DROP DATABASE DatabaseName

Drop a Table

DROP TABLE TableName

Drop a Constraint

ALTER TABLE TableName
DROP CONSTRAINT ConstraintName

Dropping a column

ALTER TABLE Users
DROP COLUMN Email;

The keyword "COLUMN" is used as part of the syntax to indicate that you are dropping a column.

EDIT

To edit an existing column, you can use the ALTER TABLE statement with the ALTER COLUMN clause.

Changing Data Type

```
ALTER TABLE Users
ALTER COLUMN FirstName NVARCHAR(255);
```

Modifying

Some modifications to database objects, like altering certain column properties or constraints, may necessitate dropping the existing object. Afterward, the ADD keyword is used to recreate it with the desired changes.

ALTER considerations

When making changes to columns in a database table, there are potential challenges and considerations to keep in mind. Here are some common problems and issues that may arise:

Data Loss: Altering a column's data type or dropping a column can result in data loss if the new data type is not compatible with the existing data or if the column contains important information that will be discarded.

Default Values: Adding a default value to an existing column can be problematic if the existing data violates the new default constraint. This might require updating existing rows to comply with the new default value.

Nullability Changes: Changing the nullability of a column, especially making a column non-nullable, can be challenging if there are existing null values. You may need to provide default values or update existing rows to eliminate null values.

Foreign Key Constraints: Modifying or dropping a column involved in a foreign key relationship can be tricky. Ensure that you update or drop the foreign key constraints before making changes to the referenced columns.

Indexes and Performance: Adding or removing columns can impact the performance of existing indexes. Be mindful of the indexes on the table and evaluate whether they need to be modified or rebuilt after column changes.

Renaming Columns: Renaming a column might have implications on stored procedures, views, or application code that reference the old column name. Make sure to update all dependent objects.

Primary Key Changes: Changing the primary key, especially dropping or altering it, can be challenging. Ensure that the primary key change doesn't impact other tables with foreign key references.

Transaction Size: Large tables with millions of rows may take a significant amount of time to modify. Ensure that you consider the transaction size and potential impact on database performance.

Data Migration: Altering a table often involves migrating existing data to conform to the new structure. This can be a resource-intensive process, especially for large tables.

Dependencies: Be aware of dependencies on the table, such as views, stored procedures, or functions that reference the table. Changes may require updates to these dependent objects.

Concurrency: Altering a table can lock the table temporarily, potentially affecting concurrent operations. Plan such modifications during low-traffic periods to minimize disruptions.

Alias

Aliases are used to provide alternative names for tables and columns in a query.

You can use the "AS" keyword for aliasing tables and columns. The "AS" keyword is optional in many situations but can be used to provide aliases to tables and columns, improving readability and making your SQL queries more expressive.

```
SELECT (u.FirstName + ' ' + u.LastName) AS FullName
FROM Users AS u
```

AS u - is the alias assigned to the table.

AS FullName - assigns the alias "FullName" to the result of the concatenation.

	FullName
1	Eldar Cohen
2	David Cohen
3	Mike Nike

Without AS word:

```
SELECT (u.FirstName + ' ' + u.LastName) FullName
FROM Users u
```

Readability: Aliases make queries more readable, especially in complex queries or when dealing with multiple tables.

Conciseness: Aliases can reduce the amount of typing needed, improving the overall conciseness of your SQL code.

Avoiding Ambiguity: When a query involves multiple tables with similar column names, aliases help to avoid ambiguity by clearly indicating the source of each column.

COMPRESSION

The WITH (DATA_COMPRESSION = PAGE) clause is used to specify the data compression method for a table or an index.

```
CREATE TABLE YourTable
(
    Column1 INT,
    Column2 VARCHAR(50)
)
WITH (DATA_COMPRESSION = PAGE);
```

Types of data compression methods

NONE: No compression is applied.

ROW: Row-level compression is applied. This compression method is designed to reduce storage space by encoding repeating values within a row.

PAGE: Page-level compression is applied. This compression method works at the page level and includes the benefits of row-level compression. Page compression is more aggressive and can achieve higher compression ratios but may involve more CPU overhead during data access.

NONE (for partitioned tables): For partitioned tables, you can choose to apply no compression to specific partitions while applying compression to others.

ORDER BY

The ORDER BY clause is used to sort the result set of a query based on one or more columns. It allows you to control the order in which the rows are presented in the query result.

Ascending Order

```
SELECT *
FROM Users
ORDER BY FirstName
```

	UserId	FirstName	LastName
1	2	David	Cohen
2	1	Eldar	Cohen
3	3	Mike	Nike

We are selecting all columns (*) from the Users table and ordering the result set based on the values in the FirstName column in ascending order (the default order is ascending, so ASC is implied). This means the result set will contain all rows from the Users table, and those rows will be sorted in alphabetical order based on the values in the FirstName column.

If you want to make the ordering explicit, you can use the ASC (ascending) keyword in the ORDER BY clause.

```
SELECT *
FROM Users
ORDER BY FirstName ASC
```

Descending Order

```
SELECT *
FROM Users
ORDER BY FirstName DESC
```

This query retrieves all columns (*) from the Users table and orders the result set based on the values in the FirstName column in descending order (DESC). This means the result set will contain all rows from the Users table, and those rows will be sorted in reverse alphabetical order based on the values in the FirstName column.

	UserId	FirstName	LastName
1	3	Mike	Nike
2	1	Eldar	Cohen
3	2	David	Cohen

Query based on more columns

This provides a two-level sorting criteria for the result set.

```
SELECT *
FROM Users
ORDER BY FirstName DESC, LastName ASC
```

The query retrieves all data from the Users table and sorts the results by two criteria.

	UserId	FirstName	LastName
1	3	Mike	Nike
2	1	Eldar	Cohen
3	2	David	Cohen

FirstName in descending order: This means the results will be sorted alphabetically by the first name of the users, with "Z" coming first and "A" coming last.

LastName in ascending order: Within each group of users with the same first name, the results will be sorted alphabetically by the last name of the users, with "A" coming first and "Z" coming last.

In essence, this query organizes the users' data alphabetically, first by first name and then by last name, starting with the last name and moving towards the first name.

SELECT without specifying an ORDER BY clause

When you select rows from a table without specifying an ORDER BY clause, the database engine does not guarantee any specific order for the result set. The order in which the rows are returned is dependent on various factors, such as the storage structure of the table, available indexes, and execution plan chosen by the query optimizer. In practice, the order of the rows may appear to be in the order they were inserted or based on the physical storage structure, but this is not guaranteed. It's crucial to understand that the default order is essentially arbitrary and can change based on factors like database maintenance, updates, or optimizations.

DISTINCT

The DISTINCT keyword is used in a SELECT statement to eliminate duplicate rows from the result set. It considers only unique values for the specified columns in the SELECT clause.

	Id	Name
1	1	Apple
2	2	Banana
3	3	Avocado
4	1	Apple
5	2	Avocado
6	3	Banana

```sql
SELECT DISTINCT *
FROM Furits
```

	ID	Name
1	1	Apple
2	2	Avocado
3	2	Banana
4	3	Avocado
5	3	Banana

Nesting SELECT statements

Nesting SELECT statements refers to the practice of using one or more SELECT statements within another SELECT statement. This can be done for various reasons, such as retrieving data from multiple tables, performing calculations on the result set, or filtering data based on certain conditions. Nesting SELECT statements is a powerful feature that allows you to create complex queries and obtain the information you need in a structured way.

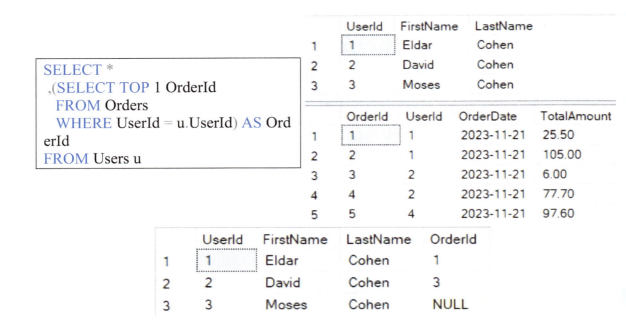

Retrieving all columns from the "Users" table and including a subquery to get the top "OrderId" for each user from the "Orders" table.

Operators

SQL Server supports a variety of operators that are used for performing operations on data in SQL queries.

Arithmetic Operators

Arithmetic operators allow you to perform basic mathematical operations on numeric values.

+ (Addition)

- (Subtraction)

* (Multiplication)

/ (Division)

% (Modulo) - the remainder of a division

The (+) and (-) operators can also be used to run arithmetic operations on datetime and small datetime.

```sql
SELECT column1 + column2 AS sum_result,
    column1 - column2 AS difference,
    column1 * column2 AS product,
    column1 / column2 AS quotient,
    column1 % column2 AS modulus
FROM your_table;
```

```sql
SELECT 2 + 1 -- 3
SELECT 2 - 1 -- 1
SELECT 2 * 2 -- 4
SELECT 4 / 2 -- 2
SELECT 3 % 2 -- 1
```

Equality/Assignment operator

While the equality operator (=) is commonly used in SQL for comparison purposes, the equal sign (=) is also used as an assignment operator.

```
DECLARE @var INT = 5;  -- assignment

SELECT *
FROM Users
WHERE UserId = 1 -- equality
```

Bitwise Operators

Bitwise operators are used to perform bit-level operations on integer expressions.

&   Bitwise AND

| Bitwise OR

^   Bitwise exclusive OR

>>   Right Shift

<<   Left Shift

```
DECLARE @value1 INT = 5;  -- Binary: 101
DECLARE @value2 INT = 3;  -- Binary: 011

SELECT @value1 & @value2 -- 1

SELECT @value1 | @value2 -- 7

SELECT @value1 ^ @value2 – 6

SELECT 3 >> 1  -- 1

SELECT 3 << 1 -- 6
```

Compound Operators

Compound operators are shorthand combinations of arithmetic and assignment operators. They allow you to perform an operation and assignment in a single statement.

+=   Add Assignment

-=   Subtract Assignment

*=   Multiply Assignment

/=   Divide Assignment

%=   Modulus Assignment

&=   Bitwise AND Assignment

^-=   Bitwise exclusive Assignment

|*=   Bitwise OR Assignment

```
DECLARE @x int = 3
SET @x+=1
SELECT @x -- 4

SET @x-=1
SELECT @x -- 3

SET @x*=2
SELECT @x -- 6

SET @x/=2
SELECT @x -- 3

SET @x%=2
SELECT @x – 1

SET @x&=3
SELECT @x -- 1

SET @x|=1
SELECT @x -- 1

SET @x^=2
SELECT @x -- 3
```

Comparison Operators

Comparison operators are used to compare values and return a Boolean result.

=	Equal to
>	Greater Than
<	Less Than
>=	Greater Than or Equal To
<=	Less Than or Equal To
<>	Not Equal To
!=	Not Equal To
!<	Not Less Than
!>	Not Greater Than

```
SELECT column1, column2
FROM your_table
WHERE column1 > column2 AND column1 <> 0;
```

Concatenation Operator

The concatenation operator is used to concatenate (combine) two or more strings into a single string. The concatenation operator is represented by the plus sign (+).

```
SELECT first_name + ' ' + last_name AS full_name
FROM Users;
```

```
SELECT 'Eldar' + ' ' + 'Cohen' -- Eldar Cohen
```

Unary operators

Unary operators are operators that operate on a single operand or expression.

Positive (+): Used to indicate a positive value. It doesn't change the sign of a positive number but is often used for clarity.

```
SELECT +10 -- 10
```

Negative (-): Used to negate the value of an expression, making it negative.

```
SELECT -5 -- -1
```

Bitwise NOT (~): Used to invert the bits of an integer expression.

```
SELECT ~5 -- -6
```

ARITHABORT

The SET ARITHABORT ON statement is used to control the behavior of how the database engine handles arithmetic overflow and divide-by-zero errors. When ARITHABORT is set to ON, it means that if an arithmetic error occurs during the execution of a statement, the entire statement is terminated, and an error is raised.

SET ARITHABORT ON

With SET ARITHABORT ON, the database engine will raise an error and terminate the query or batch if an arithmetic error, such as overflow or divide-by-zero, occurs during the execution of a statement.

SET ARITHABORT OFF

If ARITHABORT is set to OFF, the database engine will handle arithmetic errors by returning a NULL value or an approximate value rather than raising an error and terminating the statement.

IS

The IS operator is used in combination with NULL to check for null values. It is commonly used in the WHERE clause of a SELECT, UPDATE, or DELETE statement.

This query retrieves rows where column3 is NULL:

```
SELECT column1, column2
FROM your_table
WHERE column3 IS NULL;
```

This query retrieves rows where column3 is not NULL.:

```
SELECT column1, column2
FROM your_table
WHERE column3 IS NOT NULL;
```

This query retrieves rows where column3 is TRUE. Similarly, you can use FALSE.

```
SELECT column1, column2
FROM your_table
WHERE column3 IS TRUE;
```

You can use various expressions with IS to check conditions based on your requirements.

```
SELECT column1, column2
FROM your_table
WHERE column3 IS (expression);
```

The IS operator is particularly useful for handling NULL values, as standard comparison operators (=, !=, <, >, etc.) do not work as expected with NULL. For example, NULL = NULL is not true, you need to use IS NULL instead.

Logical Operators

Logical operators are used to combine or negate conditions in a query.

UserId	Salary	FirstName	LastName		OrderId	UserId	OrderDate	TotalAmount
1	1000	Eldar	Cohen		1	1	2023-11-21	25.50
2	2000	David	Cohen		2	1	2023-11-21	105.00
3	3000	Moses	Cohen		3	2	2023-11-21	6.00
					4	2	2023-11-21	77.70
					5	4	2023-11-21	97.60

AND

Returns true only if all the conditions are true.

```
SELECT *
FROM Users
WHERE Salary > 1000 AND Salary < 3000
```

UserId	Salary	FirstName	LastName
2	2000	David	Cohen

OR

returns true if at least one of the conditions is true

```
SELECT *
FROM Users
WHERE Salary <= 1000 OR Salary <= 2000
```

UserId	Salary	FirstName	LastName
1	1000	Eldar	Cohen
2	2000	David	Cohen

66

NOT

Reverses the value of any other Boolean operator.

```
SELECT *
FROM Users
WHERE NOT(Salary <= 1000)
```

UserId	Salary	FirstName	LastName
2	2000	David	Cohen
3	3000	Moses	Cohen

BETWEEN

Used to check if a value is within a specified range.

```
SELECT *
FROM Users
WHERE Salary BETWEEN 1000 AND 2000
```

UserId	Salary	FirstName	LastName
1	1000	Eldar	Cohen
2	2000	David	Cohen

You can use with dates range:

```
WHERE OrderDate BETWEEN '2023-01-01' AND '2023-12-31'
```

IN

The IN operator is used to filter the result set based on a specified list of values. It allows you to specify multiple values in a WHERE clause to include rows where the specified column matches any value in the list.

```
SELECT *
FROM Users
WHERE UserId IN (2,3)
```

UserId	Salary	FirstName	LastName
2	2000	David	Cohen
3	3000	Moses	Cohen

The IN operator is not limited to numeric values, it can also be used with string values

```
SELECT *
FROM Users
WHERE FirstName IN ('Eldar')
```

UserId	Salary	FirstName	LastName
1	1000	Eldar	Cohen

With query nesting:

```
SELECT *
FROM Orders o
WHERE UserId IN (SELECT UserId
        FROM Users
            WHERE UserId = o.UserId)
```

OrderId	UserId	OrderDate	TotalAmount
1	1	2023-11-21	25.50
2	1	2023-11-21	105.00
3	2	2023-11-21	6.00
4	2	2023-11-21	77.70

ANY/SOME

ANY and SOME are used interchangeably and have the same functionality.

Evaluate if any values returned by a subquery satisfy the condition.

Syntax:

```
SELECT column_name(s)
FROM table_name
WHERE column_name operator ALL
  (SELECT column_name
  FROM table_name
  WHERE condition);
```

```
SELECT *
FROM Users u
WHERE UserId = ANY (SELECT UserId
        FROM Orders)

SELECT *
FROM Users u
WHERE UserId = SOME (SELECT UserId
        FROM Orders)
```

UserId	Salary	FirstName	LastName
1	1000	Eldar	Cohen
2	2000	David	Cohen

ALL

Evaluate if all values returned by a subquery satisfy the condition.

Syntax:

```
SELECT column_name(s)
FROM table_name
WHERE column_name operator ALL
  (SELECT column_name
  FROM table_name
  WHERE condition);
```

```
SELECT *
FROM Users u
WHERE LastName = ALL(SELECT LastName
         FROM Users)
```

UserId	Salary	FirstName	LastName
1	1000	Eldar	Cohen
2	2000	David	Cohen
3	3000	Moses	Cohen

EXISTS

Used to check if a subquery returns any rows.

Syntax:

```
SELECT column_name(s)
FROM table_name
WHERE EXISTS
(SELECT column_name FROM table_name WHERE condition);
```

```
SELECT *
FROM Users u
WHERE Exists(SELECT UserId
        FROM Orders)
```

UserId	Salary	FirstName	LastName
1	1000	Eldar	Cohen
2	2000	David	Cohen
3	3000	Moses	Cohen

LIKE

Used in a WHERE clause to search for a specified pattern in a column.

```
SELECT *
FROM Users
WHERE FirstName LIKE 'Eldar'
```

UserId	Salary	FirstName	LastName
1	1000	Eldar	Cohen

Wildcard characters

Wildcard characters are special symbols that are used in conjunction with the LIKE operator in the WHERE clause to perform pattern matching within strings.

Percentage (%)

Represents zero or more characters.

The query is retrieving all rows from the "Users" table where the "FirstName" column begins with 'E'.

```
SELECT *
FROM Users
WHERE FirstName LIKE 'E%'
```

UserId	Salary	FirstName	LastName
1	1000	Eldar	Cohen

The query is retrieving all rows from the "Users" table where the "FirstName" column contains the letter 'a'

```
SELECT *
FROM Users
WHERE FirstName LIKE '%a%'
```

UserId	Salary	FirstName	LastName
1	1000	Eldar	Cohen
2	2000	David	Cohen

Underscore (_)

Represents a single character.

This query would match names, where the name starts with 'E', followed by 3 characters, and ending with 'r'.

```
SELECT *
FROM Users
WHERE FirstName LIKE 'E___r'
```

UserId	Salary	FirstName	LastName
1	1000	Eldar	Cohen

Square Brackets ([])

Represents any single character within the brackets.

This query retrieves users with first names starting with either 'E or 'M'.

```
SELECT *
FROM Users
WHERE FirstName LIKE '[EM]%'
```

UserId	Salary	FirstName	LastName
1	1000	Eldar	Cohen
3	3000	Moses	Cohen

Caret (^)

Represents any character not in the brackets.

This query retrieves users with first names that do not start with either 'E or 'M'.

```
SELECT *
FROM Users
WHERE FirstName LIKE '[^EM]%'
```

UserId	Salary	FirstName	LastName
2	2000	David	Cohen

Hyphen (-)

Represents any single character within the specified range.

This query retrieves all rows from the "Users" table where the "FirstName" column starts with any character in the range 'A' to 'E'. So it matches names that begin with 'A', 'B', 'C', 'D', or 'E'.

```
SELECT *
FROM Users
WHERE FirstName LIKE '[A-E]%'
```

UserId	Salary	FirstName	LastName
1	1000	Eldar	Cohen
2	2000	David	Cohen

Special characters/Escape

Special characters have a special meaning within SQL syntax or require special handling to include them in SQL statements. Some common special characters in SQL include:

Single Quote ('): Used to delimit string literals in queries. If you need to include a single quote within a string, you typically escape it by doubling it ('').

```
SELECT 'It's a good goat' -- Error
```

SQL Server will interpret the single quote within 'It' as the end of the string literal, and the subsequent characters (s a goat goat') will be considered invalid syntax.

You need to escape it by doubling it up.

```
SELECT 'It''s a good goat' -- result: It's a good goat
```

Backslash (\) (in some contexts): While not commonly used as an escape character in SQL Server itself, it can be used as an escape character in certain scenarios, such as within the LIKE operator when specifying an escape character.

Percent Sign (%) and Underscore (_) in LIKE Operator: These are special characters used in conjunction with the LIKE operator for pattern matching. % matches any sequence of characters, while _ matches any single character.

```
SELECT *
FROM MyTable
WHERE MyColumn LIKE '%\_%' ESCAPE '\';
```

This query searches for rows in the MyTable table where the MyColumn column contains a % character followed by an underscore _. The escape character \ is specified, indicating that the underscore should be treated literally rather than as a wildcard character. So, this query will return rows where MyColumn contains %_.

```
SELECT *
FROM MyTable
WHERE MyColumn LIKE '%\%%' ESCAPE '\';
```

Similarly, this query searches for rows in the MyTable table where the MyColumn column contains a % character followed by another % character. The escape character \ is specified again, indicating that the second % should be treated literally. So, this query will return rows where MyColumn contains %%

Set operators

Set operators are used to combine the result sets of two or more queries.

UNION

The UNION operator is used to combine the result sets of two or more SELECT statements. It returns a combined result set that contains distinct rows from both queries.

	ID	Name		ID	Name
1	1	Apple	1	1	Apple
2	2	Banana	2	2	Avocado
3	3	Avocado	3	3	Banana

```
SELECT * FROM Table1
UNION
SELECT * FROM Table2
```

	ID	Name
1	1	Apple
2	2	Avocado
3	2	Banana
4	3	Avocado
5	3	Banana

UNION ALL

If you want to include duplicate rows in the result set, you can use UNION ALL.

	ID	Name		ID	Name
1	1	Apple	1	1	Apple
2	2	Banana	2	2	Avocado
3	3	Avocado	3	3	Banana

```
SELECT * FROM Table1
UNION ALL
SELECT * FROM Table2
```

	ID	Name
1	1	Apple
2	2	Banana
3	3	Avocado
4	1	Apple
5	2	Avocado
6	3	Banana

EXCEPT

The EXCEPT keyword (or MINUS in some databases) is used in a SELECT statement to retrieve distinct rows from the result set of the first query that are not present in the result set of the second query. The EXCEPT operator is similar to the set operation of subtraction.

	ID	Name		ID	Name
1	1	Apple	1	1	Apple
2	2	Banana	2	2	Avocado
3	3	Avocado	3	3	Banana

```
SELECT * FROM Table1
EXCEPT
SELECT * FROM Table2
```

	Id	Name
1	2	Banana
2	3	Avocado

INTERSECT

The INTERSECT operator is used to retrieve the common rows between two result sets. It returns distinct rows that are present in both result sets. The columns in the SELECT clauses of both queries must be of the same data type and in the same order.

	ID	Name		ID	Name
1	1	Apple	1	1	Apple
2	2	Banana	2	2	Avocado
3	3	Avocado	3	3	Banana

```
SELECT * FROM Table1
INTERSECT
SELECT * FROM Table2
```

	Id	Name
1	1	Apple

Common functions in query's

	UserId	FirstName	LastName
1	1	Eldar	Cohen
2	2	David	Cohen
3	3	Moses	Cohen

COUNT

Counts the number of rows.

```
SELECT COUNT(*) AS RowsCount
FROM Users
```

RowsCount

3

```
SELECT COUNT(UserId) AS RowsCount
FROM Users
```

RowsCount

3

SUM

Calculates the sum of values.

```
SELECT SUM(UserId) AS TotalSum
FROM Users
```

TotalSum

6

AVG

Computes the average of values.

```
SELECT AVG(UserId) AS AverageResult
FROM Users
```

AverageResult

2

81

MIN

Retrieves the minimum value.

```
SELECT MIN(UserId) AS MINResult
FROM Users
```

MINResult
1

MAX

Retrieves the maximum value.

```
SELECT MAX(UserId) AS MAXResult
FROM Users
```

MAXResult
3

ABS

Calculate the absolute value of a numeric column.

```
SELECT ABS(column_name) AS AbsoluteValue
FROM YourTable;
```

SQRT

Calculate the square root of a numeric column

```
SELECT SQRT(column_name) AS SquareRoot
FROM YourTable;
```

ROUND

Round a numeric column to 2 decimal places.

```
SELECT ROUND(column_name, 2) AS RoundedValue
FROM YourTable;
```

CEILING

Round up to the nearest integer for a numeric column.

```
SELECT CEILING(column_name) AS CeilingValue
FROM YourTable;
```

FLOOR

Round down to the nearest integer for a numeric column.

```
SELECT FLOOR(column_name) AS FloorValue
FROM YourTable;
```

LEN

Get the length of a string column.

```
SELECT LEN(column_name) AS StringLength
FROM YourTable;
```

UPPER

Convert a string column to uppercase.

```
SELECT UPPER(column_name) AS Uppercase
FROM YourTable;
```

LOWER

Convert a string column to lowercase.

```
SELECT LOWER(column_name) AS Lowercase
FROM YourTable;
```

LEFT

Extract the leftmost 3 characters from a string column.

```
SELECT LEFT(column_name, 3) AS LeftSubstring
FROM YourTable;
```

RIGHT

Extract the rightmost 3 characters from a string column.

```
SELECT RIGHT(column_name, 3) AS RightSubstring
FROM YourTable;
```

LTRIM

Remove only leading spaces from a string column

```
SELECT LTRIM(column_name) AS TrimmedLeftString
FROM YourTable;
```

RTRIM

Remove only trailing spaces from a string column.

```
SELECT RTRIM(column_name) AS TrimmedRightString
FROM YourTable;
```

CHARINDEX

The CHARINDEX function is used to find the starting position of a substring within a string. If the substring is not found, it returns 0.

CHARINDEX(substring, string [, start_location])

substring: The substring you want to find within the string.

string: The string in which you want to search for the substring.

start_location (optional): The starting position for the search within the string. If not specified, the search starts from the beginning of the string.

```
SELECT CHARINDEX('eldar', 'Hi Eldar') -- 4
```

CHARINDEX is case-insensitive by default. If you need a case-sensitive search, you can use the COLLATE clause

```
SELECT CHARINDEX('eldar', 'Hi Eldar' COLLATE Latin1_General_CS_AS) -- 0
SELECT CHARINDEX('Eldar', 'Hi Eldar' COLLATE Latin1_General_CS_AS) -- 4
```

COLLATE

The COLLATE clause is used to specify the collation for a particular expression or column. Collation refers to the rules that determine how string comparison and sorting are performed. It includes considerations such as case sensitivity, accent sensitivity, and the ordering of characters.

SQL Server supports various collations, and some common ones include:

SQL_Latin1_General_CP1_CI_AS: Case-insensitive, accent-sensitive.

SQL_Latin1_General_CP1_CS_AS: Case-sensitive, accent-sensitive.

Latin1_General_CI_AS: Case-insensitive, accent-sensitive (general Latin collation).

OFFSET/FETCH/RAWS/ONLY

In SQL Server, the OFFSET and FETCH clauses are used for paging and implementing skip/take functionality. These clauses are typically used in conjunction with the ORDER BY clause to define the sort order of the result set.

Id
1
2
3
4
5
6

```
SELECT *
FROM NumberTable
ORDER BY Id
OFFSET 2 ROWS  -- skip 2 rows
FETCH NEXT 2 ROWS ONLY; --take 2 rows
```

Id
3
4

OFFSET 2 ROWS skips the first 2 rows.

FETCH NEXT 2 ROWS ONLY retrieves the next 2 rows after the offset.

```
SELECT *
FROM NumberTable
ORDER BY Id
OFFSET 4 ROWS  -- skip 4 rows
FETCH NEXT 2 ROWS ONLY; --take 2 rows
```

Id
5
6

Joins

Joins are used to combine rows from two or more tables based on a related column between them.

```sql
CREATE TABLE Users (
    UserId BIGINT PRIMARY KEY IDENTITY(1,1),
    FirstName NVARCHAR(50),
    LastName NVARCHAR(50),
);

CREATE TABLE Orders (
    OrderId INT PRIMARY KEY IDENTITY(1,1),
    UserId BIGINT,
    OrderDate DATE,
    TotalAmount DECIMAL(10, 2)
);
```

```sql
SELECT * FROM Users
SELECT * FROM Orders
```

	UserId	FirstName	LastName
1	1	Eldar	Cohen
2	2	David	Cohen
3	3	Moses	Cohen

	OrderId	UserId	OrderDate	TotalAmount
1	1	1	2023-11-21	25.50
2	2	1	2023-11-21	105.00
3	3	2	2023-11-21	6.00
4	4	2	2023-11-21	77.70
5	5	4	2023-11-21	97.60

INNER JOIN

Returns only the rows where there is a match in both tables based on the specified condition.

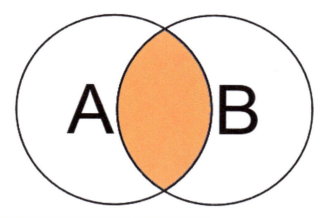

```
SELECT *
FROM Users u
INNER JOIN Orders o ON u.UserId = o.UserId
```

	UserId	FirstName	LastName	OrderId	UserId	OrderDate	TotalAmount
1	1	Eldar	Cohen	1	1	2023-11-21	25.50
2	1	Eldar	Cohen	2	1	2023-11-21	105.00
3	2	David	Cohen	3	2	2023-11-21	6.00
4	2	David	Cohen	4	2	2023-11-21	77.70

The result is all the columns from both the Users and Orders tables for the rows.

The INNER JOIN keyword combines rows from both tables where there is a match in the specified join condition. In this example, it retrieves rows where the UserId in the Users table matches the UserId in the Orders table.

ON u.UserId = o.UserId: This is the join condition. It specifies how the two tables should be connected. In this case, the join is based on the UserId column, which is assumed to be a common key between the Users and Orders tables.

The ON keyword is used in the context of the JOIN clause to specify the condition that determines how two tables are related.

The INNER keyword is optional. If you omit it, it will still perform an inner join.

```
SELECT *
FROM Users u
JOIN Orders o ON u.UserId = o.UserId
```

SELF JOIN

Joins a table with itself. Useful when working with hierarchical data or when comparing rows within the same table.

```
SELECT *
FROM Users u1
JOIN Users u2 ON u1.UserId = u2.UserId
```

	UserId	FirstName	LastName	UserId	FirstName	LastName
1	1	Eldar	Cohen	1	Eldar	Cohen
2	2	David	Cohen	2	David	Cohen
3	3	Moses	Cohen	3	Moses	Cohen

Shorthand notation (.*)

```
SELECT u.FirstName, o.*
FROM Users u
INNER JOIN Orders o ON u.UserId = o.UserId
```

	FirstName	OrderId	UserId	OrderDate	TotalAmount
1	Eldar	1	1	2023-11-21	25.50
2	Eldar	2	1	2023-11-21	105.00
3	David	3	2	2023-11-21	6.00
4	David	4	2	2023-11-21	77.70

The o.* in the SELECT statement refers to all columns (* means all columns) from the table Orders, which is aliased as o. This notation is a shorthand way of saying "select all columns from the Orders table."

LEFT (OUTER) JOIN/LEFT INCLUSIVE

Returns all rows from the left table and the matched rows from the right table. If there is no match, NULL values are returned for columns from the right table.

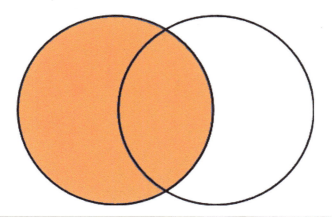

```
SELECT *
FROM Users u
LEFT JOIN Orders o ON u.UserId = o.UserId
```

	UserId	FirstName	LastName	OrderId	UserId	OrderDate	TotalAmount
1	1	Eldar	Cohen	1	1	2023-11-21	25.50
2	1	Eldar	Cohen	2	1	2023-11-21	105.00
3	2	David	Cohen	3	2	2023-11-21	6.00
4	2	David	Cohen	4	2	2023-11-21	77.70
5	3	Moses	Cohen	NULL	NULL	NULL	NULL

```
SELECT *
FROM Users u
LEFT OUTER JOIN Orders o ON u.UserId = o.UserId
```

Term "OUTER" is optional. Both LEFT JOIN and LEFT OUTER JOIN are interchangeable and mean the same thing. The keyword "OUTER" is not required but can be included for clarity.

The term "OUTER" in the context of joins, such as LEFT OUTER JOIN or RIGHT OUTER JOIN, refers to including unmatched rows from one or both of the tables involved in the join. The term "OUTER" helps to distinguish these types of joins from the more common INNER JOIN, which only returns rows that have matching values in both tables.

LEFT EXCLUSIVE

A "LEFT EXCLUSIVE" operation, achieved through a LEFT JOIN with a condition in the WHERE clause, retrieves all records from the left table and includes only those that do not have corresponding matches in the right table.

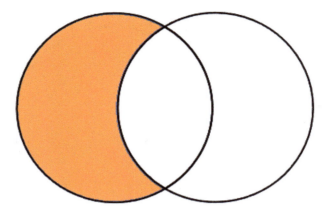

```
SELECT *
FROM Users u
LEFT JOIN Orders o ON u.UserId = o.UserId
WHERE o.UserId IS NULL
```

	UserId	FirstName	LastName	OrderId	UserId	OrderDate	TotalAmount
1	3	Moses	Cohen	NULL	NULL	NULL	NULL

RIGHT (OUTER) JOIN/RIGHT INCLUSIVE

Returns all rows from the right table and the matched rows from the left table. If there is no match, NULL values are returned for columns from the left table.

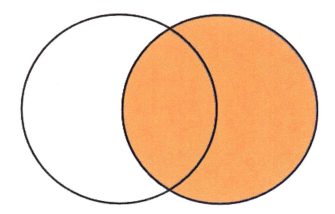

	UserId	FirstName	LastName	OrderId	UserId	OrderDate	TotalAmount
1	1	Eldar	Cohen	1	1	2023-11-21	25.50
2	1	Eldar	Cohen	2	1	2023-11-21	105.00
3	2	David	Cohen	3	2	2023-11-21	6.00
4	2	David	Cohen	4	2	2023-11-21	77.70
5	NULL	NULL	NULL	5	4	2023-11-21	97.60

RIGHT EXCLUSIVE

Returns all rows from the right table and includes only those that do not have corresponding matches in the left table.

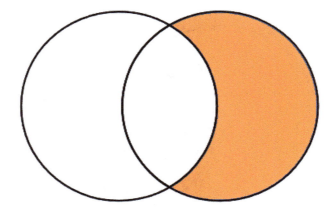

```
SELECT *
FROM Users u
RIGHT JOIN Orders o ON u.UserId = o.UserId
WHERE u.UserId IS NULL
```

	UserId	FirstName	LastName	OrderId	UserId	OrderDate	TotalAmount
1	NULL	NULL	NULL	5	4	2023-11-21	97.60

FULL (OUTER) JOIN/ FULL INCLUSIVE

Returns all rows when there is a match in either the left or the right table. If there is no match, NULL values are returned for columns from the table without a match.

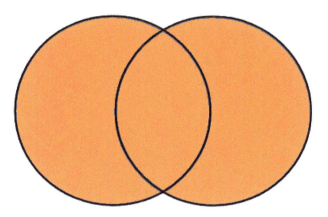

```
SELECT *
FROM Users u
FULL JOIN Orders o
ON u.UserId = o.UserId
```

	UserId	FirstName	LastName	OrderId	UserId	OrderDate	TotalAmount
1	1	Eldar	Cohen	1	1	2023-11-21	25.50
2	1	Eldar	Cohen	2	1	2023-11-21	105.00
3	2	David	Cohen	3	2	2023-11-21	6.00
4	2	David	Cohen	4	2	2023-11-21	77.70
5	3	Moses	Cohen	NULL	NULL	NULL	NULL
6	NULL	NULL	NULL	5	4	2023-11-21	97.60

FULL EXCLUSIVE

Returns all rows when there isn't a match in either the left or the right table.

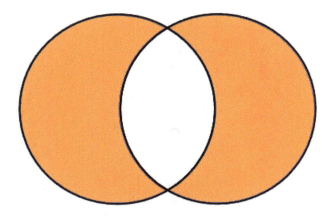

```
SELECT *
FROM Users u
FULL JOIN Orders o ON u.UserId = o.UserId
WHERE u.UserId IS NULL OR o.UserId IS NULL
```

	UserId	FirstName	LastName	OrderId	UserId	OrderDate	TotalAmount
1	3	Moses	Cohen	NULL	NULL	NULL	NULL
2	NULL	NULL	NULL	5	4	2023-11-21	97.60

The OR operator is a logical operator used to combine multiple conditions in a WHERE clause. It returns true if at least one of the conditions is true.

CROSS JOIN

CROSS JOIN is used to combine every row from the first table with every row from the second table, resulting in a Cartesian product. It does not require a specific condition.

A Cartesian product is a mathematical operation that returns a set from multiple sets by considering all possible ordered pairs of elements.

```
SELECT *
FROM Users
CROSS JOIN Orders
```

	UserId	FirstName	LastName	OrderId	UserId	OrderDate	TotalAmount
1	1	Eldar	Cohen	1	1	2023-11-21	25.50
2	1	Eldar	Cohen	2	1	2023-11-21	105.00
3	1	Eldar	Cohen	3	2	2023-11-21	6.00
4	1	Eldar	Cohen	4	2	2023-11-21	77.70
5	1	Eldar	Cohen	5	4	2023-11-21	97.60
6	2	David	Cohen	1	1	2023-11-21	25.50
7	2	David	Cohen	2	1	2023-11-21	105.00
8	2	David	Cohen	3	2	2023-11-21	6.00
9	2	David	Cohen	4	2	2023-11-21	77.70
10	2	David	Cohen	5	4	2023-11-21	97.60
11	3	Moses	Cohen	1	1	2023-11-21	25.50
12	3	Moses	Cohen	2	1	2023-11-21	105.00
13	3	Moses	Cohen	3	2	2023-11-21	6.00
14	3	Moses	Cohen	4	2	2023-11-21	77.70
15	3	Moses	Cohen	5	4	2023-11-21	97.60

APPLY

The APPLY operator is used to invoke a table-valued function for each row returned by an outer table expression. It allows you to join a table-valued function with other tables and apply the function to each row of the outer table.

	UserId	Salary	FirstName	LastName
1	2	2000	David	Cohen
2	3	3000	Moses	Cohen
3	4	NULL	2	2
4	5	NULL	3	3

	OrderId	UserId	OrderDate	TotalAmount
1	1	1	2023-11-21	25.50
2	2	1	2023-11-21	105.00
3	3	2	2023-11-21	6.00
4	4	2	2023-11-21	77.70
5	5	4	2023-11-21	97.60

CROSS APPLY

It returns only the rows from the outer table that produce a result set from the table-valued function. If the table-valued function returns an empty result set for a specific row in the outer table, that row will not be included in the final result.

Both CROSS APPLY and INNER JOIN are used when you want to retrieve only the rows that have matching values in both tables or result sets. If the function or subquery in CROSS APPLY produces an empty result set for a specific row in the outer table, that row will not be included in the final result, similar to how an INNER JOIN only returns matched rows.

```
SELECT *
FROM Users u
CROSS APPLY (SELECT *
       FROM Orders o
       WHERE o.UserId = u.UserId) sub
```

	UserId	Salary	FirstName	LastName	OrderId	UserId	OrderDate	TotalAmount
1	2	2000	David	Cohen	3	2	2023-11-21	6.00
2	2	2000	David	Cohen	4	2	2023-11-21	77.70
3	4	NULL	2	2	5	4	2023-11-21	97.60

OUTER APPLY

It returns all rows from the outer table, even if the table-valued function returns an empty result set for some rows. If the function returns a result set, the columns from the function are included in the result set; otherwise, NULL values are returned.

Both OUTER APPLY and LEFT JOIN are used when you want to retrieve all rows from the left (outer) table, and if the function or subquery produces an empty result set for a specific row, NULL values are returned for the columns of the function, similar to how a LEFT JOIN returns unmatched rows with NULL values for columns from the right table.

```sql
SELECT *
FROM Users u
OUTER APPLY (SELECT *
        FROM Orders o
        WHERE o.UserId = u.UserId) sub
```

	UserId	Salary	FirstName	LastName	OrderId	UserId	OrderDate	TotalAmount
1	2	2000	David	Cohen	3	2	2023-11-21	6.00
2	2	2000	David	Cohen	4	2	2023-11-21	77.70
3	3	3000	Moses	Cohen	NULL	NULL	NULL	NULL
4	4	NULL	2	2	5	4	2023-11-21	97.60
5	5	NULL	3	3	NULL	NULL	NULL	NULL

GROUP BY

The GROUP BY clause is used to group rows based on the values of one or more columns. It is often used in conjunction with aggregate functions to perform calculations on each group of rows.

The query retrieves the user ID and the corresponding order count for each user.

```sql
SELECT u.UserId, COUNT(o.OrderId) AS OrderCount
FROM Users u
LEFT JOIN Orders o ON u.UserId = o.UserId
GROUP BY u.UserId
```

	UserId	OrderCount
1	1	2
2	2	2
3	3	0

GROUP BY u.UserId: This clause groups the results by the 'UserId' column, effectively summarizing the order counts for each unique user.

COUNT(o.OrderId): function that calculates the total number of non-null values in the OrderId column. It provides a valuable metric for understanding the overall volume of orders.

GROUP BY RULES

1. All fields in the GROUP BY clause must appear in the SELECT clause.

2. Any non-grouped fields must be aggregated using an aggregate function. This rule ensures that the results are consistent and unambiguous.

Aggregate functions are used to perform a calculation on a set of values and return a single value. These functions operate on a group of rows and produce a single result for each group.

HAVING

The HAVING clause is used to filter the results of a query that includes a GROUP BY clause. It allows you to apply conditions to the aggregated data resulting from the GROUP BY operation. The HAVING clause is particularly useful when you want to filter the results based on aggregate functions, such as COUNT, SUM, AVG, MIN, or MAX.

```
SELECT u.UserId, SUM(o.TotalAmount) as TotalAmount
FROM Users u
JOIN Orders o ON u.UserId = o.UserId
GROUP BY u.UserId
HAVING SUM(o.TotalAmount) > 90
```

	UserId	TotalAmount
1	1	130.50
2	2	83.70

The HAVING clause filters the results to include only those users whose total order amount is greater than 90.

The SUM() function is an aggregate function that is used to calculate the sum of values in a numeric column. It is used to calculate the sum for each group of rows.

Clause's order

In a typical SQL query, the clauses are generally used in the following order:

```
SELECT
    column1,
    column2,
    aggregate_function(column3) AS aggregated_column
FROM
    table1
JOIN
    table2 ON table1.columnX = table2.columnY
WHERE
    condition1 AND condition2
GROUP BY
    column1, column2
HAVING
    aggregate_function(column3) > value;
```

SELECT: Specifies the columns to be retrieved in the result set.

FROM: Specifies the table or tables from which to retrieve the data.

JOIN: Specifies how to combine rows from different tables based on a related column between them.

WHERE: Filters the rows based on a specified condition.

GROUP BY: Groups the result set by one or more columns.

HAVING: Filters the result set based on conditions applied to the groups created by the GROUP BY clause.

Query clauses logical order

The logical order of the SQL query clauses does not necessarily reflect the order in which the clauses are executed. The actual order of execution is determined by the SQL query optimizer, which aims to find the most efficient execution plan for retrieving the data.

The general logical order of the clauses is as follows:

FROM: Specifies the tables or views from which to retrieve the data.

JOIN: Specifies how to combine rows from different tables.

WHERE: Filters the rows based on specified conditions.

GROUP BY: Groups the result set based on one or more columns.

HAVING: Filters the result set based on conditions applied to the groups.

SELECT: Specifies the columns to be included in the result set.

ORDER BY: Sorts the result set based on specified columns.

However, the actual execution order might differ. The SQL Server query optimizer analyzes the query and generates an execution plan that takes into account factors such as indexes, statistics, and the structure of the underlying tables. The optimizer may choose to reorder operations to optimize performance.

Query optimizer

The SQL Server query optimizer is a component of SQL Server responsible for generating efficient execution plans for SQL queries. Its primary goal is to find the most efficient way to retrieve the requested data based on the available indexes, statistics, and the structure of the database.

Query Parsing: The query optimizer first parses the SQL query and generates a query tree, representing the logical operations specified in the query.

Query Optimization: The optimizer explores different execution plans and estimates the cost associated with each plan.

It considers factors such as table scan vs. index seek, join algorithms, and the order of operations.

The goal is to minimize the overall cost, where cost is typically measured in terms of I/O, CPU, and memory usage.

Cost-Based Optimization: SQL Server uses a cost-based optimization model. It estimates the cost of each possible execution plan and chooses the plan with the lowest estimated cost.

The cost estimation is based on statistics about the distribution of data in tables, the presence of indexes, and other factors.

Statistics: Statistics provide information about the distribution of data in tables and indexes.

The query optimizer uses statistics to make informed decisions about the most efficient way to retrieve data.

Caching: SQL Server caches execution plans to avoid re-optimizing the same queries repeatedly.

If a similar query is executed, the optimizer may reuse the cached execution plan if the underlying data or schema has not changed significantly.

Hints: Developers can provide hints in queries to guide the optimizer's decision-making process. However, it's generally recommended to let the optimizer make decisions unless there's a specific need for manual intervention.

Plan Caching: SQL Server maintains a plan cache to store execution plans for frequently executed queries. This helps in reusing plans and avoiding unnecessary recompilations.

Recompilation: The optimizer might recompile a query when there are changes to the underlying tables, indexes, or certain query-related options. Recompilation ensures that the optimizer has the most up-to-date information for making optimization decisions.

BEGIN/END Blocks

BEGIN and END are used to define a block of statements. All statements between BEGIN and END are treated as a single unit and are executed together if the condition specified in the IF statement is true.

```
BEGIN
--Your code
END
```

IF

The IF statement is used to conditionally execute a block of SQL statements. It evaluates a condition and, if the condition is true, the statements within the BEGIN and END block are executed, otherwise, they are skipped.

```
IF(@param1 = NULL)
BEGIN
 RETURN
END
```

IFF

IIF is a shorthand for a conditional expression that returns one of two values depending on the evaluation of a Boolean expression.

Syntax: IIF(condition, value_if_true, value_if_false)

```
SELECT IIF(5 > 3, 'True', 'False') -- True
```

PRINT

The PRINT statement is used to display messages in the messages pane. This can be useful for debugging, providing feedback, or displaying informational messages during the execution of a script or a batch of statements.

```
PRINT 'Hello';
```

Messages
```
Hello
```

IF/ELSE

The IF...ELSE statement is used for conditional execution of code blocks. The IF...ELSE statement is a control-of-flow statement that allows you to execute different blocks of code based on a specified condition.

```
DECLARE @Salary INT = 2500;

IF @Salary BETWEEN 2000 AND 3000
  BEGIN
    PRINT 'Medium Earner';
  END

ELSE IF @Salary > 3000
  BEGIN
    PRINT 'Big Earner';
  END

ELSE
  BEGIN
    PRINT 'Low Earner';
  END
```

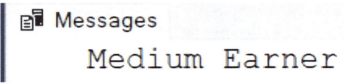

If the @Salary is between 2000 and 3000 (inclusive), 'Medium Earner' will be printed.

If the @Salary is greater than 3000, 'Big Earner' will be printed.

If neither of the above conditions is met, 'Low Earner' will be printed.

This structure allows you to create a tiered categorization of earners based on salary ranges. The ELSE IF statements provide additional conditions to check if the previous conditions are not met.

CASE

The CASE statement is used to perform conditional logic within a query. It allows you to conditionally execute a set of statements based on one or more conditions.

The query is using the CASE statement to create a new column named BigEarner based on the salary conditions. The column BigEarner will be set to 1 if the salary is greater than or equal to 3000, and it will be set to 0 if the salary is less than or equal to 2999.

```
SELECT UserId
,(CASE
   WHEN Salary >= 3000 THEN 1
   WHEN Salary <= 2999 THEN 0
   ELSE 0
END) BigEarner
FROM Users
```

UserId	BigEarner
1	0
2	0
3	1

WHEN condition **THEN** result: This part is where you specify the condition that needs to be met. If the condition is true, then the result corresponding to that condition is returned.

ELSE: This part is optional. If none of the conditions are true, the ELSE clause provides a default result. If omitted and no conditions are true, the result is NULL.

END: Indicates the end of the CASE statement.

CAST

The CAST function is used to explicitly convert an expression of one data type to another. It is particularly useful when you need to convert data from one type to another, such as converting a string to a numeric type or vice versa.

Syntax: CAST (expression AS data_type)

```
SELECT CAST('15' AS INT) – 15

SELECT CAST(25 AS DECIMAL(5,2)) -- 25.00

SELECT CAST('2023-01-15' AS DATE) -- 2023-01-15

SELECT CAST('AS' AS INT) -- Conversion failed when converting the varchar value 'AS' to data type int.
```

TRY_CAST

the TRY_CAST function is used to attempt to cast a value to a specified data type. If the cast is successful, it returns the casted value; otherwise, it returns NULL. This function is particularly useful when you want to avoid errors that would occur if a direct cast is attempted and the conversion is not possible.

```
SELECT TRY_CAST('2023-01-15' AS DATE) -- 2023-01-15

SELECT TRY_CAST('AS' AS CHAR) -- AS

SELECT TRY_CAST('AS' AS INT) -- NULL
```

CONVERT

The CONVERT function is used to convert an expression from one data type to another. It's similar to the CAST function but provides more flexibility, especially when dealing with date and time conversions where you can specify a format.

Syntax: CONVERT (data_type , expression [, style])

Style - An optional integer expression that specifies how the conversion should be performed, particularly in the case of date and time conversions. The style parameter determines the format of the result.

```
SELECT CONVERT(NVARCHAR(30), GETDATE(), 120)
-- Ouput: 2023-11-24 03:22:04
```

When you use 120 as the style in the CONVERT function, it formats the date and time as follows:

YYYY: Four-digit year

MM: Two-digit month (01-12)

DD: Two-digit day of the month (01-31)

HH: Two-digit hour in 24-hour format (00-23)

MI: Two-digit minute (00-59)

SS: Two-digit seconds (00-59)

More styles: https://learn.microsoft.com/en-us/sql/t-sql/functions/cast-and-convert-transact-sql

Functions used to handle NULL values

ISNULL

ISNULL is a function that replaces NULL with the specified replacement value.

Syntax: ISNULL(expression, replacement_value)

```
SELECT ISNULL(null, 'DefaultValue') -- DefaultValue

SELECT ISNULL(3, 'DefaultValue') -- 3
```

COALESCE

COALESCE returns the first non-NULL expression among its arguments. It is more flexible than ISNULL because it can take multiple parameters.

Syntax: COALESCE(expression1, expression2, ..., expressionN)

```
SELECT COALESCE(1, 2, 'DefaultValue') -- 1

SELECT COALESCE(null, 2, 'DefaultValue') -- 2

SELECT COALESCE(null, null, 'DefaultValue') – DefaultValue

SELECT COALESCE(null, null, null) -- error
At least one of the arguments to COALESCE must be an
expression that is not the NULL constant.
```

110

Table Variables

Both table variables and temporary tables are used to store and manipulate data temporarily during the execution of a batch, stored procedure, or function. However, there are some differences between the two.

Table Variable

Declaration: Table variables are declared using the DECLARE statement, similar to other variables.

```
DECLARE @Users TABLE (
    UserId BIGINT PRIMARY KEY,
    Salary BIGINT,
    FirstName NVARCHAR(50),
    LastName NVARCHAR(50)
)
```

Populate @Users with the data from Users table with INSERT INTO statement:

```
INSERT INTO @Users
SELECT * FROM Users
```

```
SELECT * FROM @Users
```

UserId	Salary	FirstName	LastName
1	1000	Eldar	Cohen
2	2000	David	Cohen
3	3000	Moses	Cohen

Scope: Table variables have a limited scope and are only visible within the batch, stored procedure, or function where they are declared.

Lifetime: The lifetime of a table variable is limited to the duration of the batch, stored procedure, or function.

Transaction Scope: Table variables are always in the scope of the transaction that surrounds the code using them.

Indexing: Table variables do not support non-clustered indexes.

Temporary Table

Declaration: Temporary tables are created using the CREATE TABLE statement with a prefix # for local temporary tables or ## for global temporary tables.

```sql
CREATE TABLE #Users ( -- temporary table
   UserId BIGINT PRIMARY KEY,
   Salary BIGINT,
   FirstName NVARCHAR(50),
   LastName NVARCHAR(50)
)

INSERT INTO #Users
SELECT * FROM Users
```

```sql
CREATE TABLE ##Users ( -- global temporary table
   UserId BIGINT PRIMARY KEY,
   Salary BIGINT,
   FirstName NVARCHAR(50),
   LastName NVARCHAR(50)
)

INSERT INTO ##Users
SELECT * FROM Users
```

Scope: Local temporary tables (#) are only visible within the session that created them.

Global temporary tables (##) are visible across all sessions but are dropped when the creating session is closed.

Lifetime: Local temporary tables are dropped automatically when the session that created them ends. Global temporary tables persist until all sessions referencing them are closed.

Transaction Scope: Temporary tables can be used across transactions.

Indexing: Temporary tables support non-clustered indexes, providing more indexing options.

SELECT INTO #Table

This syntax creates a temporary table and populates it with the result set of a SELECT statement in a single step. The columns and their data types in the temporary table are automatically determined based on the columns in the SELECT statement. It is a concise way to create a temporary table and populate it with data in one go.

```
SELECT *
INTO #tempTable
FROM Users

SELECT *
FROM #tempTable
```

The SELECT INTO #tempTable statement creates a temporary table named #tempTable and copies the entire result set (all columns and rows) from the Users table into this temporary table.

The second SELECT * FROM #tempTable statement retrieves all columns from the #tempTable temporary table.

DROP TABLE

DROP TABLE #tempTable statement is used to explicitly drop (delete) the temporary table named #tempTable. This action removes the temporary table and its data from the current session.

```
DROP TABLE #tempTable
```

It's a good practice to explicitly drop temporary tables when they are no longer needed to free up resources and avoid clutter in the temporary object space. Temporary tables are automatically dropped when the session ends, but it's a best practice to clean up after yourself when you're done using them explicitly.

Temporary tables vs Global temporary tables

Feature	Temporary Tables	Global Temporary Tables
Visibility	Private to the current session	Visible to all sessions in the current instance of SQL Server
Scope	Local to the current session	Global to all sessions in the current instance of SQL Server
Deletion	Deleted when the session ends	Deleted when all sessions that have referenced the table have closed
Creation	`CREATE TABLE #tableName` syntax	`CREATE TABLE ##tableName` syntax
Use cases	Storing intermediate results of a query or procedure	Sharing data between sessions or storing data that is needed for a longer period of time

Table variables vs Temporary tables

Feature	Table Variables	Temporary Tables
Scope	Local to the current scope	Global within the session
Storage	Memory	tempdb database
Visibility	Accessible only within the scope of declaration	Accessible by multiple procedures or batches in the session
Data size	Suitable for small to moderate amounts of data	Can handle larger amounts of data
Creation	DECLARE @tableName TABLE syntax	CREATE TABLE #tempTable syntax
Performance	Generally faster for small datasets	May be slower for large datasets due to I/O operations
Transactional behavior	Not affected by transaction rollbacks	Affected by transaction rollbacks

WITH

The WITH clause is used to create temporary result sets, often referred to as Common Table Expressions (CTEs). A CTE allows you to define a temporary result set. The CTE have a limited scope and is only available within the execution of the query in which they are defined. Once the query execution is complete, the CTE is no longer accessible.

```sql
WITH cte_users (id, fullName) AS (
    -- CTE definition
    SELECT UserId, FirstName + ' ' + LastName
    FROM Users
)
-- SQL statement that references the CTE
SELECT *
FROM cte_users;

-- cte_users no longer accessible
```

you can use multiple CTEs within the same WITH clause, separating them with commas.

```sql
WITH cte_users (id, fullName) AS (
    SELECT UserId, FirstName + ' ' + LastName
    FROM Users
),cte_users2 (id) AS (
    SELECT id
    FROM cte_users
)

SELECT *
FROM cte_users
JOIN cte_users2
ON cte_users.id = cte_users2.id
```

TRY/CATCH

The TRY...CATCH block is a mechanism for error handling. It allows you to gracefully handle errors that may occur during the execution of a batch of SQL statements. The TRY block contains the statements that might generate an error, and the CATCH block contains the code that will be executed if an error occurs.

```sql
BEGIN TRY
   -- Statements that might cause an error
END TRY
BEGIN CATCH
   -- Handling code for the error
END CATCH
```

```sql
BEGIN TRY
   DECLARE @Result INT;
   SET @Result = 1 / 0; -- This will cause a divide by zero error
END TRY
BEGIN CATCH
   PRINT 'error: ' + ERROR_MESSAGE();
END CATCH
```

🗔 Messages

```
    error: Divide by zero error encountered.
```

The TRY block contains a division operation that will cause a divide-by-zero error.

If an error occurs, the control is transferred to the CATCH block.

The CATCH block contains code to handle the error. In this case, it prints an error message using the ERROR_MESSAGE() function.

The ERROR_MESSAGE() function is a system function that returns the error message text generated by the last statement executed.

Functions for additional information about errors

```sql
BEGIN TRY
   SELECT 1 / 0;
END TRY
BEGIN CATCH
  PRINT 'An error occurred:';
  PRINT 'Error Number: ' + CAST(ERROR_NUMBER() AS NVARCHAR(10));
  PRINT 'Error Severity: ' + CAST(ERROR_SEVERITY() AS NVARCHAR(10));
   PRINT 'Error State: ' + CAST(ERROR_STATE() AS NVARCHAR(10));
   PRINT 'Error Procedure: ' + ISNULL(ERROR_PROCEDURE(), '');
   PRINT 'Error Line: ' + CAST(ERROR_LINE() AS NVARCHAR(10));
END CATCH
```

```
An error occurred:
Error Number: 8134
Error Severity: 16
Error State: 1
Error Procedure:
Error Line: 3
```

ERROR_NUMBER(): Returns the error number of the last message in the session. The error number uniquely identifies the error.

ERROR_SEVERITY(): Returns the severity level of the last error in the session. Severity levels range from 0 to 25, with lower values indicating less severe errors and higher values indicating more severe errors.

ERROR_STATE(): Returns the state or location code of the last error in the session. It's an integer between 0 and 255.

ERROR_PROCEDURE(): Returns the name of the stored procedure or trigger where the error occurred. If the error did not occur within a stored procedure or trigger, this function returns NULL.

ERROR_LINE(): Returns the line number in the batch, stored procedure, or trigger where the error occurred.

RAISEERROR

The RAISEERROR statement is used to generate an error message and to initiate error processing. It can be used to explicitly raise a user-defined error within a batch, stored procedure, or trigger.

Syntax: RAISERROR ({ msg_id | msg_str | @local_variable } { , severity, state } [, argument [, ...n]]) [WITH option [, ...n]]

```
BEGIN TRY
   IF (Condition1 is NULL OR Condition2 is NULL)
   BEGIN
      -- Raise error if conditions are not met
      RAISEERROR('parameters must have values.', 16, 1);
   END
END TRY
BEGIN CATCH
   PRINT 'error: ' + ERROR_MESSAGE();
END CATCH
```

16: Severity level of the error. 1: Is an integer that represents a state or location code within the stored procedure or batch where the error occurred.

msg_id: An integer that represents the error message ID. You can find predefined error messages in the sys.messages catalog view.

msg_str: A string that represents the custom error message.

@local_variable: A local variable containing either the message ID or the message string.

severity: An integer between 0 and 25 that indicates the severity level of the error. Severity levels 0-18 are informational or warning messages, and severity levels 19-25 are error messages.

state: An integer between 0 and 255 that represents a state or location code within the stored procedure or batch where the error occurred. It's a user-defined value.

argument [, ...n]: Optional parameters representing values to replace placeholders (%s, %d, etc.) in the error message string.

WITH option [, ...n]: Additional options that modify the behavior of the RAISEERROR statement. Options may include LOG, SETERROR, and others.

THROW

The THROW statement is used to raise an exception and transfer control to a CATCH block in a structured manner. The THROW statement is often used in conjunction with nested TRY...CATCH blocks to re-throw or propagate the exception to an outer level of error handling.

Syntax: THROW [{ error_number | @local_variable }, { message | @local_variable }, { state | @local_variable }] [;]

In this example, there are two levels of TRY...CATCH blocks. If an error occurs in the inner block, the THROW statement is used to re-throw the exception to the outer block.

```
BEGIN TRY
   BEGIN TRY
            -- Inner TRY block
      SELECT 1 / 0; -- This will cause an error
   END TRY
   BEGIN CATCH
      PRINT 'Inner CATCH block';
      -- Rethrow the inner exception to the outer level
      THROW;
   END CATCH
END TRY
BEGIN CATCH
   -- Outer CATCH block
   PRINT 'Outer CATCH block';
END CATCH
```

⊞ Results   🗗 Messages

```
Inner CATCH block
Outer CATCH block
```

You can also use THROW to raise custom exceptions by specifying an error number, message, state, and optional parameters:

```
THROW 99, 'Custom error message', 1;
```

A custom error with error number 99, message 'Custom error message', and state 1 is thrown.

Stored procedure

Stored procedures are containers of code that you can call by name. Stored procedures allow you to encapsulate a piece of logic and reuse it in various parts of your SQL code. Stored procedures are precompiled and stored sets of one or more SQL statements that are used to perform a specific task. They are similar to functions in programming languages and offer several advantages, including improved performance, code reusability, and enhanced security.

CREATE Stored procedure

```
CREATE PROCEDURE MyStoredProcedure
AS
-- SQL statements to perform the desired task
```

ALTER stored procedure

The ALTER PROCEDURE statement is used to modify an existing stored procedure.

```
ALTER PROCEDURE MyStoredProcedure
AS
-- SQL statements to perform the desired task
```

Call Stored procedure

Calling stored procedures involves using the EXEC statement followed by the name of the stored procedure and any required parameters.

```
EXEC MyStoredProcedure
```

DROP stored procedure

To remove or drop a stored procedure, you can use the DROP PROCEDURE statement.

```
DROP PROCEDURE MyStoredProcedure
```

Input parameters

Stored procedures can take input parameters, which allow you to pass values into the procedure. Input parameters are specified in the stored procedure's definition using the @ sign followed by the parameter name and data type.

```
CREATE PROCEDURE MyStoredProcedure
@param1 BIGINT,
@param2 BIGINT
AS
```

Call the stored procedure with specific parameter values:

```
EXEC MyStoredProcedure 1,2
```

Or with parameters naming:

```
EXEC MyStoredProcedure @param1 = 1, @param2 = 2
```

You must send all the input parameters, otherwise you will get an error:

```
EXEC MyStoredProcedure 1
```

Procedure or function 'MyStoredProcedure' expects parameter '@param2', which was not supplied.

Optional parameters/Default value

Optional parameters in stored procedures allow you to specify parameters that are not always required when calling the procedure. Default values can be assigned to optional parameters, and they are used if the parameter is not specified when calling the procedure.

```sql
CREATE PROCEDURE MyStoredProcedure
 @param1 BIGINT = 50
,@param2 BIGINT = NULL
AS

SELECT @param1 AS param1, @param2 as param2
```

```sql
EXEC MyStoredProcedure
EXEC MyStoredProcedure 1
EXEC MyStoredProcedure 1, 2
EXEC MyStoredProcedure @param2 = 2
```

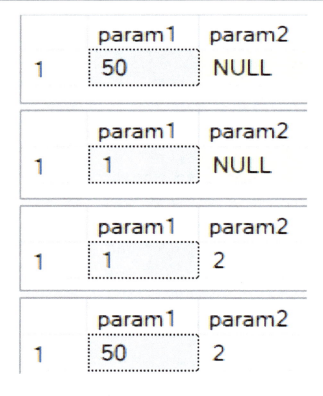

Return data with SELECT

Stored procedures can return result sets using the SELECT statement.

```
CREATE PROCEDURE MyStoredProcedure
AS

SELECT *
FROM Users
```

```
EXEC MyStoredProcedure
```

	UserId	FirstName	LastName
1	1	Eldar	Cohen
2	2	David	Cohen
3	3	Moses	Cohen

Multi select statements inside stored procedure

```
CREATE PROCEDURE MyStoredProcedure
AS
SELECT * FROM Users
SELECT * FROM Orders
```

In the stored procedure there are two SELECT statements. However, only the result of the last SELECT statement will be returned when you execute the stored procedure. In this case, it will be the result of SELECT * FROM Orders. The result of the first SELECT statement (SELECT * FROM Users) will not be returned by the stored procedure because the second SELECT statement overwrites it.

In the context of ADO.NET (ActiveX Data Objects for .NET), it is possible to retrieve multiple result sets from a stored procedure. ADO.NET supports the NextResult method of the SqlDataReader class, which allows you to navigate through multiple result sets returned by a stored procedure.

RETURN keyword

The RETURN keyword is used to control the flow of execution within a stored procedure. It can be used to:

1. Exit a stored procedure: The most common use of the RETURN keyword is to exit a stored procedure. When you use the RETURN keyword without specifying a value, it immediately exits the stored procedure and returns to the caller.

2. Return a single value from a stored procedure: The RETURN keyword can also be used to return a single value from a stored procedure. This is particularly useful for scalar values, such as counts, sums, or maximum values.

```
CREATE PROCEDURE AddNumbers
 @param1 BIGINT
,@param2 BIGINT
AS
IF(@param1 = NULL OR @param2 = NULL)
BEGIN
 RETURN --exit
END

DECLARE @result BIGINT = @param1 + @param2;

RETURN @result -- return
```

```
DECLARE @AddResult INT
EXEC @AddResult = AddNumbers @param1 = 5, @param2 =7
```

You can use the return statement inside a stored procedure to return an integer status code, of integer type only.

Output parameters

You can use output parameters to return values from stored procedures or functions. Output parameters allow you to pass values from a stored procedure or function back to the calling program or script.

The stored procedure calculates the count of users, and then you execute it, passing the @Count variable as an output parameter

```sql
CREATE PROCEDURE GetUsersCount
    @UsersCount INT OUTPUT
AS
BEGIN
    SELECT @UsersCount = COUNT(*)
    FROM Users
END;

DECLARE @Count INT;

EXEC GetUsersCount @UsersCount = @Count OUTPUT;

PRINT 'Number of Users: ' + CAST(@Count AS NVARCHAR)
```

Scope

The term "scope" in the context of stored procedures generally refers to the visibility or accessibility of variables within the stored procedure.

Local Scope

Local scope refers to the visibility of variables declared within a specific stored procedure. Variables declared within a stored procedure are only accessible within that procedure. Once the stored procedure finishes execution, the variables go out of scope, and their values are no longer accessible.

```
CREATE PROCEDURE MyProcedure
AS
BEGIN
   -- Local variable
   DECLARE @LocalVariable INT;
   SET @LocalVariable = 10;

   -- This variable is only accessible within this
   -- procedure
   -- Once the procedure completes, @LocalVariable goes
   -- out of scope
END;
```

Global Scope

Global scope, on the other hand, refers to the visibility of variables or objects that are accessible across multiple stored procedures or throughout the entire database. In SQL Server, you can use global temporary tables, session variables, or system functions to achieve a form of global scope.

```sql
-- Create a global temporary table
CREATE TABLE ##GlobalTempTable (
    ID INT
);

-- Procedure 1
CREATE PROCEDURE Procedure1
AS
BEGIN
    -- Access the global temporary table
    INSERT INTO ##GlobalTempTable (ID) VALUES (1);
END;

-- Procedure 2
CREATE PROCEDURE Procedure2
AS
BEGIN
    -- Access the global temporary table
    SELECT * FROM ##GlobalTempTable;
END;
```

Global temporary tables (prefixed with ##) are accessible across different sessions and procedures. However, they are temporary and will be automatically dropped when the last session referencing them is closed.

Function

A function is a database object that allows you to encapsulate a piece of logic and reuse it in various parts of your SQL code. There are two main types of functions, scalar functions and table-valued functions.

Multi select statements inside stored procedure are not allowed.

Scalar Functions

A Scalar Function returns a single value based on the input parameters.

```
CREATE FUNCTION MyFunction
(
    @Number1 INT,
    @Number2 INT
)
RETURNS INT
AS
BEGIN
    DECLARE @Result INT;
    SET @Result = @Number1 + @Number2;
    RETURN @Result;
END;
```

The RETURNS INT specifies the data type of the value that the function will return.

Table-Valued Functions

A Table-Valued Function returns a table result set. There are two types, inline table-valued functions and multi-statement table-valued functions.

Inline Table-Valued Function (ITVF)

The SELECT statement defines the structure and data of the table that the function returns.

ITVFs consist of a single SELECT statement, and they are generally more concise and easier to read.

```
CREATE FUNCTION MyFunction
()
RETURNS TABLE
AS
RETURN
(
    SELECT * FROM Users
);
```

Thee RETURNS TABLE specifies that the function will return a table result set.

Multi-Statement Table-Valued Function (MTVF)

MTVFs are defined with multiple statements within the RETURNS @TableVariable clause. They use a table variable to store and return the result set.

```
CREATE FUNCTION MyFunction
(
    -- Input Parameters
)
RETURNS @ResultTable TABLE
(
    FirstName NVARCHAR(50),
    LastName NVARCHAR(50)
)
AS
BEGIN
    INSERT INTO @ResultTable
    SELECT FirstName, LastName
    FROM Users
    -- Additional logic if needed
    RETURN;
END;
```

Scalar Functions vs Table-Valued Functions

Feature	Scalar Functions	Table-Valued Functions
Output	Single value	Set of rows and columns (virtual table)
Usage	Simple calculations, data transformations, validations	Complex data manipulation, filtering, aggregation, data retrieval
Scope	Local	Global
Integration	Can be used in expressions, WHERE clauses, and SELECT clauses	Can be used in FROM clauses, WHERE clauses, and SELECT clauses
Performance	Generally faster due to simpler execution	May be slower due to more complex data manipulation

Call function

```
SELECT * FROM MyFunction()
```

```
DECLARE @AddResult INT = dbo.AddFunction(5, 7);
```

DROP function

To drop a function, you can use the DROP FUNCTION statement followed by the name of the function.

```
DROP FUNCTION MyFunction
```

ALTER function

To alter a function, you can use the ALTER FUNCTION statement followed by the modifications you want to make. However, it's important to note that not all alterations are allowed and you should review the SQL Server documentation for details on what modifications can be made to a function. If a significant change is required, it might be safer to drop and recreate the function.

Stored Procedures vs Functions

Stored procedures and functions are similar, but they serve different purposes and have some key differences in their usage and behavior.

Stored Procedures

Purpose: Stored procedures are designed to perform one or more actions on the database. They can include multiple SQL statements and procedural logic.

Return Type: Stored procedures may or may not return a value. If they return a value, it is typically an integer status code indicating success or failure.

Usage: Stored procedures can be used to encapsulate a series of SQL statements, execute complex logic, and perform operations like data manipulation, transaction management, and more.

Transaction Handling: Stored procedures can include transaction control statements (BEGIN TRANSACTION, COMMIT, ROLLBACK) to manage transactions.

Output Parameters: Stored procedures can have output parameters, allowing them to return data in addition to the result set.

Permissions: Stored procedures can be granted execute permissions separately from table permissions, providing a layer of security.

Functions

Purpose: Functions are designed to return a single value or a table result set. They are used to encapsulate a specific piece of logic and can be called within SQL statements.

Return Type: Functions must return a value, and the return type is specified when the function is created.

Usage: Functions are often used in SELECT statements, WHERE clauses, and other places where a single value or set of values is required.

Transaction Handling: Functions cannot include transaction control statements. They are not intended to modify data or manage transactions.

Output Parameters: Functions can have output parameters, but their primary purpose is to return a value through the RETURN keyword.

Permissions: Functions operate under the permissions of the user calling them, and they must have appropriate permissions on the underlying tables.

Feature	Functions	Stored Procedures
Purpose	Perform a specific task and return a single value	Execute a series of SQL statements and can return multiple values or perform actions
Data modification	Cannot modify data	Can modify data
Scope	Local	Global
Return values	Single value	Multiple values or no values
Security	More secure	Less secure
Performance	Faster	Slower
Complexity	Less complex	More complex

VIEW

A view is a virtual table that is based on the result of a SELECT statement. Views allow you to encapsulate complex queries and present the results as if they were a table. They are similar to tables in that you can query them using SELECT statements, but they don't store the data themselves, instead, they represent a stored SELECT statement. Views are read-only by default. If you need to perform INSERT, UPDATE, or DELETE operations through a view, you might need to create an INSTEAD OF trigger to handle these operations.

Create view

```
CREATE VIEW MyView
AS
SELECT FirstName, LastName
FROM Users u
INNER JOIN Orders o ON u.UserId = o.UserId
```

Call view

```
SELECT * FROM MyView
```

Drop view

```
DROP VIEW MyView
```

SCHEMABINDING

SCHEMABINDING is a feature that can be applied to views and user-defined functions. When you use SCHEMABINDING on these database objects, you are essentially binding the structure of the object to the schema of the underlying tables or functions that it references.

```
CREATE VIEW MyView
WITH SCHEMABINDING
AS
SELECT FirstName, LastName
FROM Users u
INNER JOIN Orders o ON u.UserId = o.UserId
```

Dependency Check

SCHEMABINDING ensures that the underlying schema of the referenced tables or functions cannot be modified or dropped without first removing the SCHEMABINDING from the dependent objects. This helps to avoid accidental changes to the structure that could break the dependent views or functions.

Performance Optimization

SCHEMABINDING can provide performance benefits because the query optimizer can make certain assumptions about the underlying tables' structure. This can lead to more efficient query plans.

Indexed Views

If you are creating an indexed view, SCHEMABINDING is required. Indexed views store the result set of a query as a physical table, and SCHEMABINDING ensures that the view's schema remains bound to the base tables.

TRIGGER

Triggers are special types of stored procedures that are automatically executed in response to certain events on a particular table or view. Triggers are used to enforce business rules, perform custom actions, or modify data before or after specific operations, such as INSERT, UPDATE, or DELETE.

AFTER Trigger/FOR Trigger

Executed after the triggering action (INSERT, UPDATE, DELETE) has completed.

Commonly used for auditing, logging, or updating related tables.

```
CREATE TRIGGER AfterInsertTrigger
ON Users --table name
AFTER INSERT --insert action
AS
BEGIN
    -- Trigger logic after an INSERT operation
        PRINT 'User inserted'
END;
```

INSTEAD OF Trigger/Before Trigger

An INSTEAD OF trigger allows you to skip the normal execution of an INSERT, DELETE, or UPDATE statement and, instead, execute a different set of statements defined within the trigger. The actual data modification operation (insert, delete, or update) is replaced by the logic specified in the trigger.

```
CREATE TRIGGER InsteadOfInsertTrigger
ON Users
INSTEAD OF INSERT
AS
BEGIN
    -- Custom logic to handle the INSERT operation
    INSERT INTO Users (Salary, FirstName, LastName)
    SELECT
        I.Salary,
        I.FirstName,
        I.LastName
    FROM INSERTED I
    WHERE I.Salary >= 0
      AND I.FirstName <> ''
      AND I.LastName <> '';
END;
```

The INSTEAD OF INSERT trigger is defined on the Users table.

The trigger logic checks that the Salary is greater than or equal to 0, and both FirstName and LastName are not empty strings.

If these conditions are met, the trigger inserts the values into the Users table using the INSERTED virtual table.

ALTER/DROP

```
ALTER TRIGGER InsteadOfInsertTrigger
ON Users
INSTEAD OF INSERT


DROP TRIGGER InsteadOfInsertTrigger ON Users
```

Triggers impact

Triggers are attached to specific tables or views and are automatically fired when the associated events occur. It's important to use triggers judiciously, as they can introduce complexity and affect performance.

Performance Impact: Triggers can impact performance, especially if they involve complex logic or modify large amounts of data. Test triggers thoroughly to ensure they do not adversely affect performance.

Nesting: Triggers can be nested (one trigger invoking another). However, excessive nesting can lead to unexpected behavior, so it's important to manage trigger execution carefully.

Data Consistency: Triggers should be designed to maintain data consistency. For example, an INSTEAD OF trigger might be used to enforce a certain business rule before allowing an UPDATE operation to proceed.

Avoid Lengthy Operations: Avoid performing lengthy operations within triggers, as this can cause delays in the execution of the original SQL statement.

Nested triggers

Triggers can be nested, meaning that a trigger can invoke another trigger as part of its execution.

```
CREATE TRIGGER FirstTrigger
ON MyTable
AFTER INSERT
AS
BEGIN
    -- Outer trigger logic

    -- Call another trigger
    EXEC AnotherTrigger;

    -- More outer trigger logic
END
```

There are some important considerations and limitations when it comes to nested triggers:

Nested Trigger Execution: When a trigger is fired and it performs an action that fires another trigger, the second trigger is said to be nested within the first.

Nested triggers are executed in a separate scope, and the sequence of execution is determined by the order in which the triggers are defined.

Maximum Nesting Level: SQL Server imposes a limit on the nesting level of triggers. By default, the maximum nesting level is 32.

You can configure this limit using the sp_configure system stored procedure, but it is generally advisable to keep nested triggers to a minimum.

Impact on Performance: Excessive use of nested triggers can impact performance. Each trigger invocation adds to the overhead of transaction processing, and the cumulative effect can be significant. Consider the potential for infinite loops if triggers are not carefully designed, leading to poor performance and even system instability.

Avoiding Recursive Triggers: Recursive triggers occur when a trigger executes a statement that fires the same trigger again. To prevent recursive triggers, use the DISABLE TRIGGER and ENABLE TRIGGER statements or check the TRIGGER_NESTLEVEL function.

Loops

In SQL, especially in a relational database like SQL Server, the concept of loops is not as explicit as in procedural programming languages. SQL operates on sets of data and is designed to perform set-based operations efficiently. However, there are constructs and techniques that can be used to achieve looping-like behavior in SQL.

While Loop

The WHILE keyword is used to create a loop that repeats a set of statements as long as a specified condition is true.

```
DECLARE @Counter INT = 1;

WHILE @Counter <= 5
BEGIN
    -- Your code here
    PRINT 'Iteration ' + CAST(@Counter AS NVARCHAR(10));
    SET @Counter = @Counter + 1;
END;
```

Messages

```
Iteration 1
Iteration 2
Iteration 3
Iteration 4
Iteration 5
```

DECLARE @Counter INT = 1; Initializes a variable @Counter with an initial value of 1.

WHILE @Counter <= 5: Checks if the condition is true (if @Counter is less than or equal to 5). If true, the code inside the BEGIN...END block is executed; otherwise, the loop is exited.

PRINT 'Iteration ' + CAST(@Counter AS NVARCHAR(10));: Prints the current iteration number.

SET @Counter = @Counter + 1;: Increments the @Counter variable by 1.

The loop continues until @Counter becomes greater than 5.

Cursors
CURSOR/FOR/FETCH/NEXT/CLOSE/DEALLOCATE /@FETCH_STATUS

Cursors can be used to iterate through a result set row by row. However, cursors should be used with caution as they may impact performance.

```sql
DECLARE @ID INT;
DECLARE CursorName CURSOR FOR SELECT ID FROM YourTable;

OPEN CursorName;

FETCH NEXT FROM CursorName INTO @ID;
WHILE @@FETCH_STATUS = 0
BEGIN
    -- Your code here
    PRINT 'Processing ID: ' + CAST(@ID AS NVARCHAR(10));

    FETCH NEXT FROM CursorName INTO @ID;
END;

CLOSE CursorName;
DEALLOCATE CursorNam
```

DECLARE @ID INT: Declares a variable @ID to store the values retrieved from the cursor.

DECLARE CursorName CURSOR FOR SELECT ID FROM YourTable: Declares a cursor named CursorName and associates it with a SELECT statement that retrieves the ID column from the YourTable table.

OPEN CursorName: Opens the cursor to make it ready for fetching rows.

FETCH NEXT FROM CursorName INTO @ID: Fetches the first row from the cursor into the variable @ID.

WHILE @@FETCH_STATUS = 0: Checks whether the fetch was successful. If @@FETCH_STATUS is 0, the fetch was successful, and the loop is entered.

PRINT 'Processing ID: ' + CAST(@ID AS NVARCHAR(10)): Performs some operation for the current row, in this case, printing the processed ID.

141

FETCH NEXT FROM CursorName INTO @ID: Fetches the next row into the variable @ID.

The loop continues as long as there are more rows to fetch (@@FETCH_STATUS = 0).

CLOSE CursorName: Closes the cursor.

DEALLOCATE CursorName: Deallocates the cursor, releasing associated resources.

@@FETCH_STATUS is a system variable used to check the status of a fetch operation. It indicates whether the last fetch operation was successful or whether there are no more rows to fetch. The value of @@FETCH_STATUS is updated after each FETCH statement in a cursor.

Here are the possible values of @@FETCH_STATUS:

0: The fetch was successful, and there are more rows to be fetched.

-1: The fetch was successful, but there are no more rows to be fetched.

1: The fetch failed or the row was beyond the result set.

Indexes

Indexes are database objects that improve the speed of data retrieval operations on database tables. They provide a quicker way to look up data in the database, similar to the index in the back of a book that allows you to quickly find information without reading the entire book.

Types of Indexes

Clustered Index: Determines the physical order of data rows in a table. Each table can have only one clustered index.

Non-Clustered Index: Provides a separate structure that contains a sorted list of references to the rows in the table. A table can have multiple non-clustered indexes.

Create Clustered Index

Indexes can be created using the CREATE INDEX statement.

```
CREATE CLUSTERED INDEX IX_UserId ON Users(UserId);
```

A primary key automatically creates a clustered index on the specified column(s).

Create Non-Clustered Index

```
CREATE NONCLUSTERED INDEX IX_LastName ON Users(LastName);
```

A unique constraint creates a unique non-clustered index.

Without specify the word CLUSTERD or NONSCLUSTERD creates a non-clustered index by default.

```
CREATE INDEX IX_LastName ON Users(LastName);
```

Indexing Best Practices

Indexes improve read performance but may slightly slow down write operations, as indexes need to be maintained.

Create indexes on columns frequently used in WHERE clauses, JOIN conditions, and ORDER BY clauses.

Avoid creating too many indexes, as this can impact insert/update/delete performance and increase storage requirements.

Index Maintenance

Regularly monitor and maintain indexes to ensure optimal performance.

Reorganize or rebuild indexes based on fragmentation levels.

Indexing Views

Indexed views(also known as a materialized view) can improve the performance of complex queries by precalculating and storing the results of aggregations or joins.

```
CREATE VIEW MyView
WITH SCHEMABINDING
AS


CREATE UNIQUE CLUSTERED INDEX IX_MyView
ON Users(UserId);
```

Indexing Functions

Be cautious when using functions in indexed columns, as this can limit the effectiveness of indexes.

```
CREATE INDEX IX_LastNameSubstring
ON Users(SUBSTRING(LastName, 1, 3));
```

Filtered Indexes

Filtered indexes are indexes built on a subset of rows in the table. They can be useful for improving query performance on a specific subset of data.

```
CREATE INDEX IX_FilteredOrders
ON Orders(OrderDate)
WHERE OrderDate >= '2023-01-01';
```

Execution Plans

Use the execution plan to analyze how SQL Server is using indexes in query processing.

To view the execution plan for a query, you can use the SHOWPLAN or SHOWPLAN_XML options or use the SQL Server Management Studio (SSMS). Here's an example using SSMS:

Write a query, for example:

```
SELECT * FROM Users WHERE UserId = 3;
```

In SSMS, press Ctrl + M to include the actual execution plan.

Execute the query.

After execution, you'll see a new tab with the execution plan. This plan will show you how SQL Server is using indexes, performing joins, and executing other operations to fulfill the query.

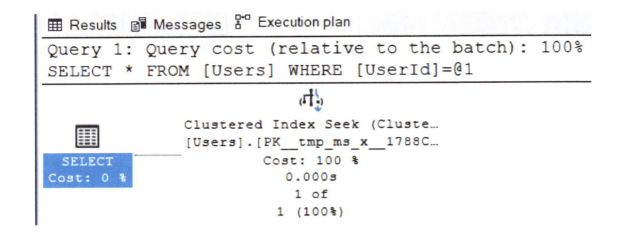

Query 1: Query cost (relative to the batch): 100%
SELECT * FROM [Users] WHERE [UserId]=@1

Clustered Index Seek (Cluste...
[Users].[PK__tmp_ms_x__1788C...
Cost: 100 %
0.000s
1 of
1 (100%)

SELECT
Cost: 0 %

Non-clustered index

A non-clustered index is a separate structure from the actual data table that is used to optimize the retrieval of data based on the values of one or more columns. Let's explore how non-clustered indexes work in SQL Server:

Index Structure: A non-clustered index is stored separately from the data table.

It is implemented as a B-tree structure (Balanced Tree) that stores the indexed column values and pointers to the corresponding rows in the data pages.

Index Key: The index key is composed of one or more columns chosen by the user when creating the index. The order of the columns in the index key determines the order of the index.

Leaf Nodes: The leaf nodes of the B-tree contain the actual index entries, which include the index key values and pointers to the corresponding rows in the data pages.

Pointers to Data: The pointers in the leaf nodes are either a reference to the physical location of the data (e.g., a row identifier) or a clustered index key if the table has a clustered index.

Data Retrieval: When a query is executed that involves the columns covered by the non-clustered index, the database engine uses the index to quickly locate the rows. The index key is used to navigate the B-tree structure, and the pointers in the leaf nodes point to the corresponding rows in the data pages.

Performance Impact: Non-clustered indexes are generally smaller in size compared to clustered indexes because they only contain the index key and pointers, not the entire data. Smaller index size can result in faster searches and better cache efficiency.

Covering Index: A covering index is a type of non-clustered index that includes all the columns required by a query. If a query can be satisfied by only accessing the non-clustered index (without the need to access the actual data pages), it is considered a covering index. Covering indexes can improve query performance by eliminating the need for additional lookups.

Sorting and Filtering: Non-clustered indexes are particularly useful for sorting and filtering operations. They allow the database engine to efficiently locate and retrieve subsets of data based on the indexed columns.

Overhead during Data Modifications: While non-clustered indexes improve query performance, they come with some overhead during data modification operations (INSERT, UPDATE, DELETE) because the indexes need to be updated along with the data.

ROLLBACK

The ROLLBACK statement is used to undo changes made in a transaction that has not been committed. It allows you to cancel the entire transaction or undo specific portions of it.

```
BEGIN TRANSACTION; -- start new transaction

-- Your SQL statements here

-- Check for some condition
IF <condition>
BEGIN
    -- Rollback the transaction if the condition is met
    ROLLBACK;
    PRINT 'Transaction rolled back.';
END
ELSE
BEGIN
    -- Commit the transaction if the condition is not met
    COMMIT;
    PRINT 'Transaction committed.';
END;
```

BEGIN TRANSACTION: Marks the beginning of a transaction. All subsequent SQL statements will be part of this transaction until it is either committed or rolled back.

COMMIT: If the transaction has executed successfully without any issues, the COMMIT statement is used to permanently save the changes made during the transaction to the database.

ROLLBACK: If an error occurs or a condition is met that requires undoing the changes made during the transaction, the ROLLBACK statement is used to revert those changes.

ROLLBACK TRAN/ROLLBACK

ROLLBACK TRAN and ROLLBACK can be used to roll back a transaction, but they have different scopes and use cases.

ROLLBACK TRAN

ROLLBACK TRAN is specifically used to roll back a named transaction.

It must be followed by the name of the transaction that you want to roll back.

It allows you to roll back a specific transaction when there are multiple transactions in progress.

```
BEGIN TRAN MyTransaction;

-- Some SQL statements

ROLLBACK TRAN MyTransaction;
```

ROLLBACK

ROLLBACK without the TRAN keyword rolls back the entire transaction associated with the current session.

It rolls back all changes made during the current transaction, regardless of whether it is explicitly named or not.

It's often used when you don't explicitly name transactions or in error-handling blocks to roll back the entire transaction.

```
BEGIN TRAN;

-- Some SQL statements

ROLLBACK;
```

@@TRANCOUNT

@@TRANCOUNT is a system function that returns the number of active transactions for the current session. It is commonly used to check the transaction count and make decisions based on whether a transaction is currently in progress.

```sql
-- Check if a transaction is in progress
IF @@TRANCOUNT > 0
BEGIN
    -- Some logic for when a transaction is in progress
    ROLLBACK; -- Rollback the transaction, for example
END
ELSE
BEGIN
    -- Some logic for when there is no active transaction
    BEGIN TRAN; -- Start a new transaction, for example
END
```

Nested Transactions

@@TRANCOUNT is incremented when a new transaction is started using BEGIN TRAN. If a transaction is rolled back (ROLLBACK TRAN), @@TRANCOUNT is decremented. Nested transactions do not affect the value of @@TRANCOUNT when they are committed or rolled back individually.

```sql
-- Example of nested transactions
BEGIN TRAN; -- @@TRANCOUNT = 1

BEGIN TRAN; -- @@TRANCOUNT = 2

-- Some SQL statements

COMMIT; -- @@TRANCOUNT = 1

ROLLBACK; -- @@TRANCOUNT = 0
```

DATETIME

In SQL Server, various functions can be used to extract or manipulate date and time information from datetime columns.

```sql
-- Get the current date and time
SELECT GETDATE() -- 2023-11-24 08:38:00.240

-- Get the current UTC date and time
SELECT GETUTCDATE() -- 2023-11-24 06:38:08.307

-- Get the month part of a date
SELECT MONTH('2023-01-15') -- 1

-- Get the day part of a date
SELECT DAY('2023-01-15') -- 15

-- Get the year part of a date
SELECT YEAR('2023-01-15') -- 2023

-- Add 3 days to the current date 2023-11-24 08:34:09.787
SELECT DATEADD(DAY, 3, GETDATE()) -- 2023-11-27 08:34:09.787

-- Add 3 year to the current date 2023-11-24 08:34:09.787
SELECT DATEADD(YEAR, 3, GETDATE()) -- 2026-11-27 08:34:09.787

-- Add 3 months to the current date 2023-11-24 08:34:09.787
SELECT DATEADD(MONTH, 3, GETDATE()) -- 2024-02-24 08:34:09.787

-- Calculate the difference in days between two dates
SELECT DATEDIFF(DAY, '2023-01-01', '2023-01-15') -- 14

-- Calculate the difference in days using DATEDIFF_BIG
SELECT DATEDIFF_BIG(DAY, '2023-01-01', '2023-01-15') --14

-- Get the last day of the month
SELECT EOMONTH('2023-01-15') --2023-01-31

-- Display the current setting for the first day of the week
SELECT @@DATEFIRST --7

-- Get the current database system timestamp
SELECT CURRENT_TIMESTAMP -- 2023-11-24 08:32:20.097

-- Construct a date value from its parts
SELECT DATEFROMPARTS(2023, 1, 15) -- 2023-01-15
```

```sql
-- Get the month name from a date
SELECT DATENAME(MONTH, '2023-01-15') -- January

-- Get the day part of a date
SELECT DATEPART(DAY, '2023-01-15') -- 15

-- Construct a datetime2 value from its parts
SELECT DATETIME2FROMPARTS(2023, 1, 15, 12, 30, 0, 0, 0)
-- 2023-01-15 12:30:00

-- Construct a datetime value from its parts
SELECT DATETIMEFROMPARTS(2023, 1, 15, 12, 30, 0, 0)
-- 2023-01-15 12:30:00.000

-- Construct a datetimeoffset value from its parts
SELECT DATETIMEOFFSETFROMPARTS(2023, 1, 15, 12, 30, 0, 0, 5, 0, 0) -- 2023-01-
15 12:30:00 +05:00

-- Construct a smalldatetime value from its parts
SELECT SMALLDATETIMEFROMPARTS(2023, 1, 15, 12, 30)
-- 2023-01-15 12:30:00

-- Truncate a date to the month
SELECT DATETRUNC(MONTH, '2023-01-15') -- 2023-01-01 00:00:00.0000000

-- Check if a value is a valid date
SELECT ISDATE('2023-01-15') -- 1

-- Change the time zone offset of a datetimeoffset value
SELECT SWITCHOFFSET('2023-01-15T12:30:00+05:00', '-08:00')
-- 2023-01-14 23:30:00.0000000 -08:00

-- Get the current date and time using the system's clock
SELECT SYSDATETIME() --2023-11-24 08:40:30.0018972

-- Get the current date and time with the time zone offset
SELECT SYSDATETIMEOFFSET() -- 2023-11-24 08:40:45.1558562 +02:00

-- Get the current UTC date and time using the system's clock
SELECT SYSUTCDATETIME() -- 2023-11-24 06:40:57.0336274

-- Convert a datetime2 value to a datetimeoffset value
SELECT TODATETIMEOFFSET('2023-01-15T12:30:00', '+05:00')
-- 2023-01-15 12:30:00.0000000 +05:00
```

More data types

HIERARCHYID

hierarchyid is a data type designed to represent position in a hierarchy or tree structure. It was introduced to support hierarchical data models, commonly used for representing organizational structures, file systems, project hierarchies, and other scenarios where items are arranged in a parent-child relationship.

The hierarchyid data type provides efficient methods for traversing and querying hierarchical data. It is particularly useful when you need to perform operations like finding the ancestors or descendants of a node, determining the level of a node in the hierarchy, or querying for a subtree.

```
CREATE TABLE EmployeeHierarchy
(
    EmployeeNode HIERARCHYID PRIMARY KEY,
    EmployeeName NVARCHAR(50)
);
```

```
-- Inserting data into the hierarchy
INSERT INTO EmployeeHierarchy (EmployeeNode, EmployeeName)
VALUES
    (hierarchyid::GetRoot(), 'CEO'),
    (hierarchyid::Parse('/1/').GetDescendant(null, null), 'CTO'), -- Child of CEO
    (hierarchyid::Parse('/2/').GetDescendant(null, null), 'CFO'), -- Another child of CEO
    (hierarchyid::Parse('/1/1/').GetDescendant(null, null), 'Manager A'), -- Child of CTO
    (hierarchyid::Parse('/1/2/').GetDescendant(null, null), 'Manager B'), -- Another child of CTO
    (hierarchyid::Parse('/2/1/').GetDescendant(null, null), 'Finance Manager'); -- Child of CFO
```

```
-- Querying hierarchy
SELECT EmployeeNode.ToString() AS EmployeePath, EmployeeName
FROM EmployeeHierarchy
ORDER BY EmployeeNode;
```

Get Ancestors:

```
SELECT EmployeeName
FROM EmployeeHierarchy
WHERE EmployeeNode.IsDescendantOf(hierarchyid::Parse('/1/')) = 1;
```

Get Descendants:

```
SELECT EmployeeName
FROM EmployeeHierarchy
WHERE EmployeeNode.GetAncestor(1) = hierarchyid::Parse('/1/');
```

Get Level:

```
SELECT EmployeeName, EmployeeNode.GetLevel() AS NodeLevel
FROM EmployeeHierarchy;
```

Updating Hierarchy:

```
UPDATE EmployeeHierarchy
SET EmployeeNode = EmployeeNode.GetDescendant(null, null)
WHERE EmployeeName = 'New Manager';
```

SQL_VARIANT

The sql_variant data type allows you to store values of different SQL Server data types as a single column. It is a flexible data type that can store a wide range of data types, and it is especially useful when you need to create a column that can hold various data types within a single table.

Flexible Storage: sql_variant columns can store values of different data types, such as integers, strings, dates, and more.

Type Coercion: SQL Server automatically performs type coercion when comparing or combining sql_variant values. This means that it can convert values to a common data type for comparison or operation.

Storage Size: The storage size of a sql_variant column depends on the specific data type of the value it contains. SQL Server allocates storage based on the actual size of the data.

Performance Considerations: While sql_variant provides flexibility, it may lead to performance issues in certain scenarios. Queries involving sql_variant columns can be slower than those using strongly-typed columns because of the additional type-checking overhead.

```sql
CREATE TABLE ExampleTable
(
    ID INT PRIMARY KEY,
    ValueColumn SQL_VARIANT
);
```

```sql
-- Select rows where ValueColumn is an integer
SELECT * FROM ExampleTable
WHERE SQL_VARIANT_PROPERTY(ValueColumn, 'BaseType') = 'int';
```

```sql
-- Select rows where ValueColumn is a string
SELECT * FROM ExampleTable
WHERE SQL_VARIANT_PROPERTY(ValueColumn, 'BaseType') = 'nvarchar';
```

```
-- Select all rows and explicitly cast ValueColumn to INT
SELECT ID, CAST(ValueColumn AS INT) AS IntValue
FROM ExampleTable;
```

```
-- Select all rows and try to cast ValueColumn to INT
SELECT ID, TRY_CAST(ValueColumn AS INT) AS IntValue
FROM ExampleTable;
```

The TRY_CAST function attempts to cast the value to the specified data type and returns NULL if the cast is not successful.

ROWVERSION

The rowversion data type, also known as timestamp, is a special-purpose data type used for versioning. It doesn't store date or time information but instead generates a unique binary number, often used to track changes in a table. When a row is inserted or updated, the rowversion column gets a new value, making it useful for identifying changes to a record.

Automatic Generation: The rowversion column is automatically updated by SQL Server when a row is inserted or updated.

Uniqueness: The rowversion values are unique within a database. However, they are not globally unique, so if you have multiple databases, each database will have its own set of unique rowversion values.

Concurrency: The rowversion is often used for optimistic concurrency control. When updating a record, you can check if the rowversion value is still the same as when you read the data. If it has changed, it indicates that someone else has modified the record in the meantime.

No Time Information: Despite the name timestamp, the rowversion data type doesn't store time information. It is purely a mechanism for versioning.

```sql
CREATE TABLE MYTable
(
  ID INT PRIMARY KEY,
  MyVal NCHAR(5),
  VersionColumn ROWVERSION
);
```

```sql
INSERT INTO MYTable (ID) VALUES (1);
SELECT * FROM MYTable;
```

ID	MyVal	VersionColumn
1	NULL	0x000000000000055F5

```sql
INSERT INTO MYTable (ID) VALUES (2);
SELECT * FROM MYTable;
```

ID	MyVal	VersionColumn
1	NULL	0x000000000000055F5
2	NULL	0x000000000000055F6

```sql
UPDATE MYTable
SET MyVal = '111'
WHERE ID = 1
SELECT * FROM MYTable;
```

	ID	MyVal	VersionColumn
1	1	111	0x000000000000055F7
2	2	NULL	0x000000000000055F6

XML

The xml data type is designed to store XML (Extensible Markup Language) data. XML is a widely used standard for representing structured data, and the xml data type enables you to store, query, and manipulate XML documents within a SQL Server database.

Storage: The xml data type stores XML data as a well-formed XML document.

Validation: The xml data type does not enforce a specific XML schema or Document Type Definition (DTD). It stores well-formed XML, but it doesn't validate against a particular structure unless explicitly specified using XML schema collections.

Methods and Functions: SQL Server provides a variety of built-in functions and methods for working with XML data. These include functions for querying, modifying, and transforming XML documents.

Indexing: SQL Server allows the creation of XML indexes on xml columns to improve the performance of XML queries.

Namespace Support: The xml data type supports XML namespaces, allowing you to work with XML documents that use namespaces.

```
CREATE TABLE MyTable
(
    ID INT PRIMARY KEY,
    XmlDataColumn XML
);
```

```
-- Inserting XML data into the table
INSERT INTO ExampleTable (ID, XmlDataColumn)
VALUES
    (1, '<Person><FirstName>Eldar</FirstName><LastName>Cohen</LastName></Person>'),
    (2, '<Person><FirstName>David</FirstName><LastName>Cohen</LastName></Person>');

    -- Querying XML data
SELECT ID,
    XmlDataColumn.value('(Person/FirstName)[1]', 'NVARCHAR(50)') AS FirstName,
    XmlDataColumn.value('(Person/LastName)[1]', 'NVARCHAR(50)') AS LastName
FROM ExampleTable;
```

GEOGRAPHY

The geography data type is used to store spatial data that represents points, lines, and polygons on the Earth's surface. This data type is part of the spatial data types introduced to support the storage and analysis of geographic information in a relational database.

Spatial Reference System: The geography data type stores data based on a spatial reference system, typically specified using the Well-Known Text (WKT) format. The spatial reference system defines the coordinate system used to represent locations on the Earth.

Geometric Types: The geography data type supports various geometric types, including points, lines, polygons, and more. You can represent complex shapes and geographic features.

Geographic Operations: SQL Server provides a wide range of built-in functions for performing operations on geography data. These operations include distance calculations, area calculations, intersection checks, and more.

Indexing: You can create spatial indexes on geography columns to improve the performance of spatial queries.

Integration with Other Technologies: SQL Server's geography data type can be used in conjunction with other technologies for mapping and visualization, such as SQL Server Reporting Services (SSRS) or Geographic Information System (GIS) applications.

```sql
CREATE TABLE LocationTable
(
    ID INT PRIMARY KEY,
    LocationColumn GEOGRAPHY
);
```

```sql
-- Inserting geographic data into the table (point)
INSERT INTO LocationTable (ID, LocationColumn)
VALUES
    (1, geography::Point(32.063051, 34.770879, 4326)),  -- tel aviv
    (2, geography::Point(32.084627, -34.832206, 4326)); -- bnei brak
```

```sql
-- Querying geographic data
SELECT ID,
    LocationColumn.STAsText() AS WellKnownText,
    LocationColumn.STDistance(geography::Point(31.776721, 35.234500
, 4326)) AS DistanceToWesternWall

FROM LocationTable;
```

The number "4326" refers to a specific Spatial Reference Identifier (SRID) that is commonly used in the context of geographic information systems (GIS) and spatial data. In SQL Server's spatial data types, the SRID is an identifier associated with a spatial object that defines the coordinate system and spatial reference system in which the object is represented.

https://learn.microsoft.com/en-us/sql/t-sql/spatial-geography/spatial-types-geography

Locks

In a relational database system, transactions use locks to control access to data in order to maintain data consistency and integrity. Shared locks are one type of lock that can be acquired by a transaction.

When a transaction acquires a shared lock on a resource (such as a row, page, or table), it indicates that the transaction is reading the resource and prevents other transactions from acquiring an exclusive lock on the same resource. However, multiple transactions can acquire shared locks on the same resource simultaneously because shared locks are compatible with other shared locks. This allows for multiple transactions to read the same data concurrently.

Blocking issues can arise when one transaction holds a lock on a resource, and another transaction is trying to acquire a conflicting lock on the same resource. In the context of shared locks, here are a few scenarios that can lead to blocking:

1. Shared Locks and Exclusive Locks Conflict:

    Transaction A acquires a shared lock on a resource.

    Transaction B attempts to acquire an exclusive lock on the same resource (e.g., for an update or delete operation).

    Transaction B is blocked until Transaction A releases its shared lock.

2. Shared Locks and Deadlocks:

    Transaction A acquires a shared lock on resource 1.

    Transaction B acquires a shared lock on resource 2.

    Transaction A later attempts to acquire a shared lock on resource 2, and Transaction B attempts to acquire a shared lock on resource 1.

    This situation can result in a deadlock, where neither transaction can proceed because each is waiting for a lock held by the other.

To mitigate blocking issues related to shared locks, it's important to design transactions carefully and consider factors such as the order in which locks are acquired, the duration of locks, and the potential for deadlocks.

WITH (NOLOCK)

The WITH (NOLOCK) hint is used to specify that a query can read a table without acquiring shared locks on it. This hint is often used to prevent blocking issues in a multi-user environment. When a transaction reads data from a table, it usually acquires shared locks to prevent other transactions from modifying the same data simultaneously. However, this can lead to blocking situations where one transaction is waiting for another to release its locks. The NOLOCK hint allows a query to read the data without waiting for other transactions to release locks. It is also known as a "dirty read" because it can potentially read uncommitted data that may be rolled back later. While using NOLOCK can improve query performance in some situations, it comes with the risk of reading inconsistent or incomplete data.

```
SELECT *
FROM TableName WITH (NOLOCK)
WHERE SomeColumn = 'SomeValue';
```

It's important to note a few considerations when using NOLOCK:

1. Dirty Reads: Using NOLOCK can result in reading uncommitted or "dirty" data. This can lead to inconsistencies in the results, especially if a transaction is in progress.

2. Uncommitted Data: The NOLOCK hint allows a query to read data even if it is in the process of being modified by another transaction. This means the data may be in an intermediate or uncommitted state.

3. Potential for Non-repeatable Reads and Phantom Reads: Due to the absence of locks, NOLOCK can lead to non-repeatable reads and phantom reads, where the result set may change between successive reads.

You don't have to use the WITH keyword, you can use only the NOLOCK keyword as syntactic sugar. Choose whichever format you find more readable or consistent with your coding style.

```
SELECT *
FROM TableName NOLOCK
WHERE SomeColumn = 'SomeValue';
```

With alias:

```
FROM TableName t (NOLOCK)
```

ANSI PADDING

ANSI_PADDING is a database-level setting that determines whether trailing blanks are padded to the full length of a column or whether they are truncated. This setting applies to both fixed-length (CHAR) and variable-length (VARCHAR) character columns.

ANSI_PADDING ON (default)

```
SET ANSI_PADDING ON;
```

Trailing blanks are padded to the full length of the column.

For example, if you have a CHAR(10) column and you insert the value 'abc' into it, SQL Server will pad it with seven additional spaces to make it a total of 10 characters.

ANSI_PADDING OFF

```
SET ANSI_PADDING OFF;
```

Trailing blanks are not padded to the full length of the column.

If you insert the value 'abc' into a CHAR(10) column with ANSI_PADDING OFF, only the actual characters 'abc' will be stored, and no additional spaces will be added.

The ANSI_PADDING setting also affects the behavior of string concatenation and comparison operations. It's important to note that the ANSI_PADDING setting applies to the session level. If you change it in a session, it affects subsequent operations in that session.

GO

The GO keyword is a batch separator used by the SQL Server Management Studio (SSMS) and other SQL Server tools.

When you're writing a script in SSMS or another tool, you can use GO to indicate the end of a batch of SQL statements. Each batch is then sent to the server for execution separately. This can be useful for various reasons:

Transaction Management: GO allows you to group sets of statements into separate transactions. For example, if you want to commit or roll back changes at a certain point in your script, you can separate the batches with GO.

Schema Changes: Some statements, like CREATE, ALTER, and DROP, can't be combined in the same batch with other types of statements. GO allows you to separate them into different batches.

Variable Scope: Variables declared in one batch are not visible to subsequent batches. So, if you declare variables in one batch and want to use them in another, you need to separate the batches with GO.

```
DECLARE @variable INT = 10
GO
SELECT @variable -- This would throw an error since

        -- @variable is not in scope
```

System Views

In SQL Server, there are several sys system views that provide information about various aspects of the database.

sys.sql_modules

The sys.sql_modules catalog view is a system view that contains information about the definition of stored procedures, triggers, functions, and views. It is part of the system catalog views and provides details about the text or definition of the modules.

```
SELECT * FROM sys.sql_modules
```

⊞ Results   ▤ Messages

	object_id	definition
1	1349579846	CREATE PROCEDURE [dbo].[AddNumbers] @param1 BI...
2	1605580758	CREATE FUNCTION MyFunction1 () RETURNS TABLE A...
3	1621580815	CREATE FUNCTION [MyFunction5] (-- Input Parameter...
4	1653580929	CREATE FUNCTION AddFunction(@a INT, @b INT) RETU...
5	1685581043	CREATE VIEW MyView2 AS SELECT FirstName, LastNam...
6	1845581613	CREATE PROCEDURE MyStoredProcedure AS SELECT ...

OBJECT_NAME/OBJECTPROPERTY

Example of how you can use sys.sql_modules to get information about stored procedures:

```sql
-- Query to retrieve information about stored procedures
SELECT
    OBJECT_NAME(object_id) AS 'ProcedureName',
    definition AS 'ProcedureDefinition'
FROM
    sys.sql_modules
WHERE
    OBJECTPROPERTY(object_id, 'IsProcedure') = 1;
```

⊞ Results 📄 Messages

	ProcedureName	ProcedureDefinition
1	AddNumbers	CREATE PROCEDURE [dbo].[AddNumbers] @param1 Bl...
2	MyStoredProcedure	CREATE PROCEDURE MyStoredProcedure AS SELECT ...

OBJECT_NAME(object_id) is used to retrieve the name of the stored procedure.

OBJECT_NAME function returns the name of a specified object based on its object ID.

OBJECTPROPERTY function returns information about a specified object, such as whether it is a table, view, stored procedure, and more.

The WHERE clause filters the results to include only procedures(IsProcedure = 1).

You can adapt this query to retrieve information about other types of modules like triggers, functions, or views by adjusting the WHERE clause accordingly (IsTrigger, IsFunction, IsView).

sys.objects

The sys.objects catalog view provides information about database objects within a SQL Server database. This view includes information about various types of objects such as tables, views, stored procedures, functions, and more.

```
SELECT * FROM sys.objects
```

▦ Results ▣ Messages

	name	object_id	principal_id	schema_id	parent_object_id	type	type_desc
1	sysrscols	3	NULL	4	0	S	SYSTEM_TABLE
2	sysrowsets	5	NULL	4	0	S	SYSTEM_TABLE
3	sysclones	6	NULL	4	0	S	SYSTEM_TABLE
4	sysallocunits	7	NULL	4	0	S	SYSTEM_TABLE
5	sysfiles1	8	NULL	4	0	S	SYSTEM_TABLE
6	sysseobjvalues	9	NULL	4	0	S	SYSTEM_TABLE
7	syspriorities	17	NULL	4	0	S	SYSTEM_TABLE
8	sysdbfrag	18	NULL	4	0	S	SYSTEM_TABLE
9	sysfgfrag	19	NULL	4	0	S	SYSTEM_TABLE
10	sysdbfiles	20	NULL	4	0	S	SYSTEM_TABLE

```
-- Query to retrieve information about user-defined tables
SELECT
    name AS 'TableName',
    type_desc AS 'ObjectType',
    create_date AS 'CreateDate',
    modify_date AS 'ModifyDate'
FROM
    sys.objects
WHERE
    type = 'U'; -- 'U' represents user-defined tables
```

▦ Results ▣ Messages

	TableName	ObjectType	CreateDate	ModifyDate
1	Addresses	USER_TABLE	2023-11-21 22:08:18.030	2023-11-23 23:39:46.303
2	Orders	USER_TABLE	2023-11-21 23:02:31.063	2023-11-21 23:02:31.070
3	Furits	USER_TABLE	2023-11-22 22:28:10.230	2023-11-22 22:28:10.230
4	Table1	USER_TABLE	2023-11-22 22:35:00.330	2023-11-22 22:35:00.330
5	Table2	USER_TABLE	2023-11-22 22:35:00.343	2023-11-22 22:35:00.343
6	NumberTable	USER_TABLE	2023-11-22 23:36:55.303	2023-11-22 23:36:55.303
7	Users	USER_TABLE	2023-11-23 23:39:46.137	2023-11-23 23:39:46.303
8	ExampleTable	USER_TABLE	2023-11-24 09:32:27.140	2023-11-24 09:32:27.140
9	MYTable	USER_TABLE	2023-11-24 09:36:58.410	2023-11-24 09:36:58.410

```
-- Query to retrieve information about stored procedures
SELECT
    name AS 'ProcedureName',
    type_desc AS 'ObjectType',
    create_date AS 'CreateDate',
    modify_date AS 'ModifyDate'
FROM
    sys.objects
WHERE
    type = 'P'; -- 'P' represents stored procedures
```

▦ Results ▩ Messages

	ProcedureName	ObjectType	CreateDate	ModifyDate
1	AddNumbers	SQL_STORED_PROCEDURE	2023-11-22 03:17:50.023	2023-11-24 05:06:29.100
2	MyStoredProcedure	SQL_STORED_PROCEDURE	2023-12-18 18:26:23.660	2023-12-18 18:26:23.660

Find all occurrences of a table

You can use a combination of system views and querying the database metadata. Below are a few queries you can use:

```
SELECT DISTINCT
    o.name AS ObjectName,
    o.type_desc AS ObjectType
FROM
    sys.sql_modules m
    JOIN sys.objects o ON m.object_id = o.object_id
WHERE m.definition LIKE '%Users%'
```

▦ Results ▩ Messages

	ObjectName	ObjectType
1	MyFunction1	SQL_INLINE_TABLE_VALUED_FUNCTION
2	MyFunction5	SQL_TABLE_VALUED_FUNCTION
3	MyStoredProcedure	SQL_STORED_PROCEDURE
4	MyView2	VIEW

sys.tables

The sys.tables system view is specifically designed to provide information about tables within a database. This view is a subset of the more general sys.objects view, focusing specifically on tables.

⊞ Results   📰 Messages

	name	object_id	principal_id	schema_id	parent_object_id	type
1	Addresses	1045578763	NULL	1	0	U
2	Orders	1269579561	NULL	1	0	U
3	Furits	1365579903	NULL	1	0	U
4	Table1	1381579960	NULL	1	0	U
5	Table2	1397580017	NULL	1	0	U
6	NumberTable	1413580074	NULL	1	0	U
7	Users	1525580473	NULL	1	0	U
8	ExampleTable	1701581100	NULL	1	0	U
9	MYTable	1749581271	NULL	1	0	U

SCHEMA_NAME

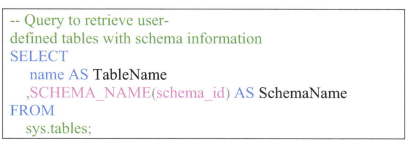

```
-- Query to retrieve user-
defined tables with schema information
SELECT
    name AS TableName
    ,SCHEMA_NAME(schema_id) AS SchemaName
FROM
    sys.tables;
```

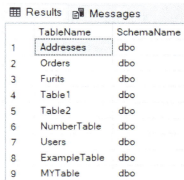

⊞ Results   📰 Messages

	TableName	SchemaName
1	Addresses	dbo
2	Orders	dbo
3	Furits	dbo
4	Table1	dbo
5	Table2	dbo
6	NumberTable	dbo
7	Users	dbo
8	ExampleTable	dbo
9	MYTable	dbo

SCHEMA_NAME function retrieves the schema name associated with the table.

INFORMATION_SCHEMA

The INFORMATION_SCHEMA is a standard schema in relational database management systems (RDBMS) that provides a set of views and tables containing metadata about the database objects within a particular database. The INFORMATION_SCHEMA is part of the SQL standard and aims to provide a consistent way to query and retrieve metadata across different database systems.

INFORMATION_SCHEMA.COLUMNS

The INFORMATION_SCHEMA.COLUMNS view provides information about columns in all tables within a database. It is part of the Information Schema, which is a standard for SQL database metadata specified by the SQL-92 standard.

```
SELECT *
FROM INFORMATION_SCHEMA.COLUMNS
```

▦ Results   ▣ Messages

	TABLE_CATALOG	TABLE_SCHEMA	TABLE_NAME	COLUMN_NAME	ORDINAL_POSITION
1	EldarDB	dbo	Addresses	UserId	1
2	EldarDB	dbo	Addresses	Street	2
3	EldarDB	dbo	Addresses	City	3
4	EldarDB	dbo	Addresses	Country	4
5	EldarDB	dbo	Orders	OrderId	1
6	EldarDB	dbo	Orders	UserId	2

Find all tables that have a certain field name

```sql
SELECT TABLE_SCHEMA,TABLE_NAME
FROM INFORMATION_SCHEMA.COLUMNS
WHERE COLUMN_NAME = 'UserId'
```

⊞ Results   ▦ Messages

	TABLE_SCHEMA	TABLE_NAME
1	dbo	Addresses
2	dbo	Orders
3	dbo	Users

INFORMATION_SCHEMA.TABLES

Contains information about tables in the database, such as table names and types.

```sql
SELECT *
FROM INFORMATION_SCHEMA.TABLES
```

⊞ Results   ▦ Messages

	TABLE_CATALOG	TABLE_SCHEMA	TABLE_NAME	TABLE_TYPE
1	EldarDB	dbo	Addresses	BASE TABLE
2	EldarDB	dbo	Orders	BASE TABLE
3	EldarDB	dbo	Furits	BASE TABLE
4	EldarDB	dbo	Table1	BASE TABLE
5	EldarDB	dbo	Table2	BASE TABLE
6	EldarDB	dbo	NumberTable	BASE TABLE
7	EldarDB	dbo	Users	BASE TABLE
8	EldarDB	dbo	MyView2	VIEW
9	EldarDB	dbo	ExampleTable	BASE TABLE
10	EldarDB	dbo	MYTable	BASE TABLE

INFORMATION_SCHEMA.VIEWS

Contains information about views in the database.

```
SELECT TABLE_NAME, VIEW_DEFINITION
FROM INFORMATION_SCHEMA.VIEWS
```

⊞ Results ⊟ Messages

	TABLE_NAME	VIEW_DEFINITION
1	MyView2	CREATE VIEW MyView2 AS SELECT FirstName, LastNa...

INFORMATION_SCHEMA.ROUTINES

Provides information about stored procedures and functions.

```
SELECT ROUTINE_NAME, ROUTINE_TYPE
FROM INFORMATION_SCHEMA.ROUTINES
```

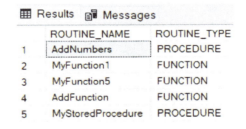

⊞ Results ⊟ Messages

	ROUTINE_NAME	ROUTINE_TYPE
1	AddNumbers	PROCEDURE
2	MyFunction1	FUNCTION
3	MyFunction5	FUNCTION
4	AddFunction	FUNCTION
5	MyStoredProcedure	PROCEDURE

INFORMATION_SCHEMA.SCHEMATA

Contains information about schemas in the database.

```sql
SELECT SCHEMA_NAME
FROM INFORMATION_SCHEMA.SCHEMATA;
```

	SCHEMA_NAME
1	dbo
2	guest
3	INFORMATION_SCHEMA
4	sys
5	db_owner
6	db_accessadmin
7	db_securityadmin
8	db_ddladmin
9	db_backupoperator
10	db_datareader
11	db_datawriter
12	db_denydatareader
13	db_denydatawriter

QUOTENAME

QUOTENAME is a built-in function that is used to properly quote or delimit a string, typically an identifier such as a column name, table name, or database name. This function is particularly useful when constructing dynamic SQL statements to prevent SQL injection and ensure that identifiers are correctly formatted.

Syntax: QUOTENAME ('character_string' [, 'quote_character'])

'character_string': This is the string that you want to quote or delimit. It can be an identifier like a column or table name.

'quote_character': This is an optional parameter specifying the character to use for quoting. The default is square brackets ([]), but you can specify a different character, such as double quotes (").

```sql
DECLARE @ColumnName NVARCHAR(50) = 'UserName';
DECLARE @QuotedColumnName NVARCHAR(100);

-- Quote the column name using QUOTENAME with default
-- square brackets
SET @QuotedColumnName = QUOTENAME(@ColumnName);

-- Result: [UserName]
PRINT @QuotedColumnName;


DECLARE @TableName NVARCHAR(50) = 'Users';
DECLARE @QuotedTableName NVARCHAR(100);

-- Quote the table name using QUOTENAME with double quotes
SET @QuotedTableName = QUOTENAME(@TableName, '"');

-- Result: "Users"
PRINT @QuotedTableName;
```

Dynamic SQL (sp_executesql)

Dynamic SQL is the creation and execution of SQL statements as strings at runtime. It allows you to build SQL statements dynamically based on certain conditions, user inputs, or other factors. Dynamic SQL can be useful in scenarios where the structure of the query is not known at compile time.

```
DECLARE @ColumnName NVARCHAR(50) = 'UserName';
DECLARE @TableName NVARCHAR(50) = 'Users';
DECLARE @DynamicSQL NVARCHAR(MAX);

-- Build the dynamic SQL statement
SET @DynamicSQL = 'SELECT ' + QUOTENAME(@ColumnName)
+ ' FROM ' + QUOTENAME(@TableName);

-- @DynamicSQL Result
-- SELECT [UserName] FROM [Users]

-- Execute the dynamic SQL statement
EXEC sp_executesql @DynamicSQL;
```

In this example, @ColumnName and @TableName are variables representing the column name and table name, respectively. The QUOTENAME function is used to properly quote the identifiers, helping to prevent SQL injection.

Use the sp_executesql system stored procedure to execute the dynamically constructed SQL statement.

@ParamDefinition

The @ParamDefinition variable in the context of using sp_executesql is used to specify the parameters and their data types that will be passed into the dynamically executed SQL query. It's essential for ensuring that the parameters are properly defined and passed to the query, helping to prevent SQL injection and ensure type safety.

```
DECLARE @SQLQuery NVARCHAR(MAX);
DECLARE @ParamDefinition NVARCHAR(MAX);
DECLARE @id INT;
DECLARE @firstName NVARCHAR(100);

-- Set the SQL query to be executed dynamically
SET @SQLQuery = N'SELECT * FROM Users WHERE id = @id AND firstName = @firstName';

-- Define parameter definitions for sp_executesql
SET @ParamDefinition = N'@id INT, @firstName NVARCHAR(100)';

-- Set parameter values
SET @id = 1;
SET @firstName = 'Eldar';

-- Execute the dynamically built SQL query
EXECUTE sp_executesql @SQLQuery, @ParamDefinition, @id, @nickName;
```